Penguin Special
The Squatters

Ron Bailey was born in 1943. Originally
a teacher, he started visiting hostels in
1964; since 1968 he has worked full-
time for the squatting movement and for
Shelter. His national report on
homelessness, entitled *The Grief
Report*, was published by Shelter at
Christmas, 1972.

Ron Bailey spends most of his time
'putting pressure on local authorities'.
He is (twice) married and has one daughter.

The Squatters

Ron Bailey

Penguin Books

Penguin Books Ltd, Harmondsworth,
Middlesex, England
Penguin Books Inc., 7110 Ambassador Road,
Baltimore, Maryland 21207, U.S.A.
Penguin Books Australia Ltd, Ringwood,
Victoria, Australia

Published in Penguin Books 1973

Copyright © Ron Bailey, 1973

Made and printed in Great Britain by
Richard Clay (The Chaucer Press) Ltd,
Bungay, Suffolk
Set in Linotype Times

Contents

1. Down and Out in the Hovels of England

Hornchurch Airfield is rather as I imagine the end of the world to be. To reach it one must journey along Suttons Lane, past Hornchurch Station, the shops, the houses, and the hospital, and then onto an unmade road which leads to the old, deserted Second World War aerodrome. The complete and utter desolation of the place is its most striking feature: the unkempt, uncared-for fields with few hedges and trees, signs of life only in the far distance, and the old stone billets that were used in the war. The whole expanse is completely at the mercy of the elements; it is the last place in which one would expect to find anybody actually living.

And yet until April 1969 the billets and huts were used as Part III Accommodation (shelter for the homeless that local authorities are obliged to provide under Part III Section 21 of the National Assistance Act of 1948) by the London Borough of Havering and a number of other neighbouring boroughs. If, on my first visit there, back in 1964, the hostel seemed to me like the end of the world, then it must have seemed doubly so to the homeless families crowded into it. This was the first hostel I had ever seen. In the course of the next six years I visited something like 150 such places, and Suttons Hostel was by no means the worst. I talked to many hundreds of people who had to strive to exist (live is far too nice a word, and certainly would give an incorrect impression that normal life is possible) in them, and one fact repeatedly struck me: if these places were not the end of the world for the occupants, they were certainly the end of the road. They were the end of normal life, the end of consideration as a human being, the end of hope, the beginning of life outside society, the beginning of social rejection and ostracism. One has to be pretty desperate to live in one of these places, and the families that are forced to are certainly that. The stigma of being labelled 'problem family', of being shunned in the shops and by hire purchase and rental firms, of being pointed at and whispered about, quite apart from the discomforts deliberately added by the 'welfare' authorities, are enough to drive away all but the most desperate.

Many only become 'problem families' when they emerge from Part III Accommodation. Three examples will serve to illustrate this. Bob Mitchell's family found themselves compelled to go to Heath Lodge, north Hertfordshire, when the owner sold the house they lived in. Bob, himself, kept his job as a builder's labourer and only visited his wife and family at weekends. However, his pay was so low that he could only manage this situation by sleeping rough himself. In the end he could stand it no longer and moved into the hostel with his family. Did that make them a 'problem family'? If so, it is worth considering whose fault it was.

My second example is the Clarke family of Birmingham. Mr and Mrs Clarke and their four children were evicted from their furnished house and had to go to the hostel at 43 Trinity Road – no husbands allowed, of course. Mr Clarke worked as hard as he could, and for as many hours as he could, in order to earn enough money for a deposit on a house. In a moment of despair he sold a rented television set to help and found himself serving a term in Winsom Green Prison. The Clarkes were then labelled a 'problem family' – once again, who was responsible?

A third illustration of the situation is to be seen in the story of the Drakes. They left Sunderland in the hope of improving their lot and moved to the south of England. But they were unhappy away from the north and Mr Drake found that work was not available. They returned to Sunderland to find that they had been crossed off the housing list because of their move. Mr Drake found a job and they all stayed with friends while he looked for a house. Eventually they could stay no longer and Mrs Drake and the children were forced to seek refuge in Highfield Lodge (another no-husband hostel). The youngest Drake child had a hole in its heart and one morning became critically ill. The hostel porter refused to allow Mrs

Drake to use the telephone in order to summon a doctor, for permission first had to be got from the warden. The warden did not arrive at the hostel until 10 a.m. – the baby died at 9 a.m. When Mr Drake arrived to visit his wife and children that evening he hit the porter and took the family away to stay with relatives for the weekend. This, however, was 'leave without permission' for Mrs Drake and so she was evicted from the hostel. The Children's Department arrived to 'offer help' and take the children into care. Fortunately, unlike so many others, the Drakes had not yet been beaten into submission. They made such a fuss that an empty house was made available to them. But that they were able to do this makes them exceptional – a more normal course would have been for the children to go into care and for the family to become a 'problem'.

The Poor Law of 1601 and the workhouses it established were abolished by the National Assistance Act of 1948. This presented all welfare authorities with a statutory obligation to provide emergency accommodation for homeless families, known as Part III Accommodation. Though the Poor Law and the workhouses were abolished in 1948, the attitudes and the establishments could not be scrapped overnight. Indeed they are still very much in existence today and not despite the newly formed 'welfare' departments, but very much because of them.

This is an extreme claim, but I can now summarize six years' travel round this country with the phrase 'down and out in the hovels of England' and I will try to convey some of my experiences in order to justify it. Let me say in advance that some of the information may be slightly out of date: it is not possible to visit every hostel every month. But enough of what follows will be sufficiently recent to show that, in general, conditions and attitudes remain largely the same today as they ever were.

Suttons Hostel was a dump; a shock to me. Long billets with bare stone walls and tiny rooms off to the side in which the families lived. Families with two or three children had one room; families with more might be lucky enough to get two rooms. And when I say they were tiny I am not exaggerating: some would hardly take a double bed; bunks were the only possibility. At the end of each billet were the communal kitchen and toilet facilities.

Many hostels had a 'welfare' office on the premises which the residents would avoid. If they complained about conditions, or the cold, or the treatment they had received, they would be called to the office. Perhaps there they would see the 'welfare' worker and get a dusting down from the officer; if they were unlucky they would be met by 'the committee' and would often emerge in tears, after having it drummed into them for half an hour how ungrateful they were for what the 'welfare' department had done for them.

It's not our fault you're here, you know, you've no one to blame for it but yourselves, you should have worked harder, shouldn't have started a family before you had saved up to buy a house, and that accident is no excuse, you should have put a few shillings away each week in case of something like that occurring, then you wouldn't have got evicted, and just because your husband threw you out that's not our fault, and even though the landlady wouldn't take you with that second child, you should have taken precautions, or exercised a bit of self-control until you'd found somewhere where they didn't mind a family. There are plenty of people who are worse off than you, there are plenty of places worse than this, where they don't allow the husbands to live-in, you know, we're liberal here, we turn a blind eye to it, although it's against the rules; we could order him out if we wanted to, now if you go back to your room we'll say no more about this matter, and by the way we don't want the press here, it hampers our work, disturbs those people we're helping, so tell them to go away if they come, because after all if you break the rules we can turn you out, and then you'll have nowhere to go and you know what that means.

'We turn a blind eye to your husband being here, but not all places are so reasonable.' An understatement that. King Hill Hostel, 1965: a billet-like place, like Suttons; a former workhouse. There they did not turn a 'blind eye' to husbands at the hostel; in fact there was a strict rule against them. Husbands were only allowed to visit during the daytime at weekends; at all other times they were forbidden to be in the hostel. Numerous other authorities made the same rule – Birmingham, Sunderland, Essex, East Sussex. Of the first three I will say

more shortly. East Sussex ran a hostel called Furze House, at
Flimwell. On 16 December 1966 the County Welfare Officer,
Mr A. J. B. Middleton, wrote to me that 'women and children
only are admitted to this accommodation'. At King Hill,
administered by the Kent County Council, the residents put up
with this rule for years, until in 1965 one husband refused to
accept it, and moved in. Others followed and the Kent County
Council Welfare Department replied by getting high court injunctions restraining the husbands from visiting the hostel out
of time. Under threat of imprisonment some men agreed to
abide by the injunctions, but then changed their minds. One
visited his wife because the children were ill and she was on
the verge of a nervous breakdown. The Welfare Department
had him jailed for 'contempt of court'. The husbands won
though and the rule was changed after a year-long struggle.
Twenty-two other authorities then changed their rules, petri-
fied that the same kind of campaign might be waged in their
hostels. Not all, however, as we shall see, have yet been 'persuaded' to do so.

'If you break the rules we can turn you out, and then you'll
have nowhere to go and you know what that means.' The
'welfare' department's final method of keeping control. Such
statements, such rules, would be enforced by social workers.
Families who 'misbehaved' would be evicted onto the streets
with their families. But not to worry, Britain's army of social
workers had control of the situation: the children would be
whisked off 'into care' and the following report might appear
in the council minutes:

After they were evicted from the hostel, as a result of not being
co-operative with the Welfare Department, the officers of the
Children's Department offered assistance to the family.

Some local authorities were not even as 'liberal' as this: they
didn't wait for a breach of the rules before they evicted a family
and took their children into care, they imposed a time limit on
the family's stay. At King Hill it was three months, and for
years an average of sixty families a year were broken up permanently because of this rule. The same letter from the East
Sussex County Welfare Officer stated 'where no accommoda-

tion has been found within three months, the children are taken into care'. At 'The Firs', Bakewell, Derbyshire, the same rule applied. Again at King Hill this rule was resisted and defeated after a year's bitter struggle. Not one social worker of the Kent County Council Welfare Department spoke out against the rule during the campaign to change it. If three months was inhuman in 1966, then the discovery by some friends of mine in 1969 that the Croydon Welfare Department imposed a *six week* time limit on homeless families' stay in their temporary accommodation, a rule they enforced until they were stopped recently, does not bear thinking about.

After all the campaigns and the public pressure over the last few years some authorities are now more subtle. While ostensibly they do not take children into care or separate families, a closer look reveals a different picture. Families who are literally homeless are actually turned away by homeless families' departments. In London, for every one homeless family that applies for temporary accommodation and receives it, five are turned away. What happens to them? Who knows? No figures are kept on this but from my own experience I know that some walk the streets, some have their children taken into care, some are 'dumped' in other boroughs, others are 'dumped' on relatives or friends who then live in fear of the council or the private landlord discovering the unlawful occupants.

Some instances of this situation make hair-raising stories: in the summer of 1970 Margaret Baker was shunted for three days between the welfare departments of Hackney, Greenwich and Lambeth; in September 1971 Bromley Welfare Department provided no temporary accommodation for the Skinners but, instead, took their children into care – until the squatters heard of the case, when the council changed its mind and offered accommodation; in Newham in September 1969 I took part in the following telephone conversation (just a short while after the 'Quartermain incidents' described in Chapter 5):

'Mr Bailey?'
'Yes.'
'East London Squatters?'
'Yes.'

'Newham Council here – we've got a homeless family here but the welfare department will not provide temporary accommodation. Will you squat them in Redbridge for us?'

I could give dozens more examples from many boroughs and from the counties of Essex, Kent and Hertfordshire. This is welfare 1971 – or social service as it is now called; but those who think that the Seebohm Report solved things ought to ask their local authority to publish the H.41 forms. These show how many homeless families apply for temporary accommodation – and how many actually get it. They make interesting reading – they are also confidential.

Birmingham, January 1967: the temperature is below zero and there is a wisp of snow in the air. I am wrapped up to the ears in scarves and pullovers, but still the cold gets through. I wait to see a woman approaching with five children trailing behind her; all look tired, depressed and half dead. I talk to her, but she can hardly speak, so frozen is her face. She had walked the streets for two and a half hours followed by her kids. The reason for this is Rule 7, Emergency Hostel Accommodation, signed J. J. Atkinson, Housing Manager:

Families will not normally be expected to remain in the hostel during the daytime in good weather, but should take the opportunity to get as much *fresh air* as weather permits. (italics in original)

This rule was enforced by Birmingham's 'social workers'. In practice this meant that in all weathers, barring snow storms, the residents were booted out of the Birmingham hostels at 2 p.m. and not allowed to return until 5.30 p.m.

Rule 10, Birmingham hostels: 'Transfer or discharge from the hostel may be made without notice.' Rule 8, Birmingham hostels: 'Children should be in bed at a time appropriate to their age, e.g. up to ten years of age by 8 p.m. The normal retiring hour at the hostel is 10 p.m.' All these rules were enforced, and indeed could not have been implemented without the full co-operation of Birmingham's welfare workers.

10 Soho Road, Handsworth, Birmingham: the kitchens were only open at certain times: 4.30 p.m.–6 p.m. for tea; 1 p.m.–2 p.m. for dinner. At other times the kitchens were

locked; if you wanted a cup of tea between these times you were unlucky ... or not quite. I spoke to the manageress of a nearby launderette where the women (no husbands allowed in the hostel, of course) would go when Rule 7 was operating. She'd make them tea, or heat up their babies' bottles. I could not help wondering what the social workers would have done had they found out. At 10 Soho Road the Birmingham City Council allowed husbands to visit between 7 p.m. and 8 p.m. weekday evenings only. They met their wives in a communal room, and the children were brought down to see them. Under no circumstances were they allowed up to their wives' rooms. If the women were living on National Assistance the husbands were not allowed to visit them. No pictures, radios, television sets or electric irons were allowed. On Sundays this rule was relaxed: radios could be played quietly! There are no locks on the doors and if the women stay in bed in the morning after getting-up time the warden would burst in and strip the covers off them. No locks on the door did I say? I must correct that: there are locks on the outside of the doors; these enable the inmates to obey the rule which says that they must lock their children in the rooms while they clean the whole place down twice a day. Margaret Mitchell[1] committed a heinous crime: she spoke to Jeremy Sandford and myself. Her punishment was to be banned from looking out of the windows; in addition she was made to scrub paint off the floor of a room on her hands and knees using steel wool.

As I've already said, the National Assistance Act of 1948 abolished the Poor Law of 1601, and the workhouses.

43 Trinity Road, Birmingham 6: the kitchens open from 7 a.m. until 10 a.m., 12 noon until 2 p.m., and from 4.30 through the night, but only for babies' bottles. If the babies want a bottle during the day when the kitchens are closed that is just unfortunate. The women (no husbands allowed) have to be in by 7.45 p.m. or else they are locked out: if that happens the children are then deemed to be in danger and are taken into care. Toilets have to be scrubbed on hands and knees; there are bars on the windows.

1. In this chapter, but not in any others, I have changed the names of the people I mention.

The Gardens, Winchester Hill, Romsey, Hampshire: I visited this establishment at the beginning of 1967. As hostels go its physical conditions are quite good and there is a reasonable amount of space for the families. I bluffed my way in by dropping the name of Mr Long, the County Welfare Officer. No husbands are allowed because homeless families 'would then make no effort to find other accommodation'. Families are not allowed to use the front entrance of the old people's home which is in the same complex of buildings. Langtry Hostel, Liverpool: this place was opened so that the old hostel, Belmont Road Workhouse, could be closed. Physical conditions good, rules not so. Rule 9: 'All visitors are required to sign the visitors book.' Heath Lodge, Royston, north Hertfordshire: ill-lit, prison-like; looks what it is, an old Victorian workhouse. Council buildings, Poplar: administered by the London Borough of Camden; we squatted families from there in 1969; you can sit on the toilet and cook your dinner; there is no hot water; the place is opposite a rubbish transfer station. Highfield Lodge, Sunderland: three and four families share one long dormitory; here, too, there is a rule about staying in during the day. South Lodge, Lane End Place, Leeds: six families live in two small rooms – a living room and a bedroom, divided into six sections like cattle stalls by wooden partitions. At 10 p.m. the families have to go to the sleeping quarters, where they are locked in until the morning; there is a toilet in the dormitory. Mr Hill, Welfare Officer for Leeds, said: 'Yes I can definitely say that the workhouse mentality has gone,' (Leeds University News, 3 March 1967).

And Abridge, Essex: 'The worst shit hole this side of hell.' The most ghastly hole of all perhaps. It is an old land army barracks built of stone. With bare walls the hostel consisted of two long rooms – a day room and a night room. Fifty people lived, and some died, in these two dormitories. They had no privacy, no separate rooms. Each family had a cubicle – 'they call us cubies because we live in cubicles,' (woman in *Cathy Come Home*). Husbands were not allowed; indeed it would have been impossible to accommodate them in the two communal dormitories; they sat on the dustbins outside and their wives handed their meals out to them; they were allowed in the hostel for eight hours on Saturdays and Sundays only. In autumn 1966 a direct action campaign closed it down.

Beechcroft Buildings in Tower Hamlets, Louise Court and Barnaby Buildings in Lambeth, Chaucer House in Southwark, Duncan House in Hackney, Council Buildings in Camden, Dartmouth Road in Brent, Plumstead Lodge in Greenwich are all tenement ghettoes for homeless families. King Hill Hostel, West Malling, Kent, much improved but still pretty awful; Scotia House, Stoke-on-Trent – no male visitors allowed, except in the communal room. All these places are still in use. Some boroughs accommodate their homeless families by giving them 'one night stands' in bed and breakfast places. This 'one night' may become days and weeks. Sometimes a borough may simply provide a family with the fare back to another part of the country, without ever enquiring whether they will have anywhere to stay when they get there.

And the people? Were they 'problem families'? work-shy? feckless? Some were; many were not to begin with, but it was a miracle if they weren't when they emerged from these places. It's beyond me to understand how the welfare officials could think that the rules and conditions they impose could possibly help families with problems. Suppose Mrs Smith did get behind with the rent? How can putting her in a dormitory help her? Suppose Mr Brown did refuse to get a job? How can separating him from his wife and taking his kids into care help him? Suppose Mrs Jones did need help with her weekly budgeting? How can those enforced 'fresh air' periods help her? Perhaps, however, they aren't meant to help. I've often thought that perhaps they're meant to teach the homeless victims not to get into difficulties again.

The twenty-one thousand people who live in Part III Accommodation are not the only sufferers in the housing crisis, however, in fact they are by far the smallest group. There are, according to the Ministry of Housing statistics, 1,800,000 families (not people) living in accommodation classed as 'unfit for human habitation'; 3,000,000 families (not people) living in slums and another 2,000,000 families living in accommodation classed as 'badly in need of repair'. This last figure is significant because these 2,000,000 units of accommodation are tomorrow's slums, and they mean that unless both the present house building rate and the slum clearance programmes are stepped up enormously, then slums will continue to grow faster than they are being cleared. So if these figures seem bad enough, just wait to see what they are like in five years' time.

The slums; the overcrowded rooms; what are they like? Take Charlie Wilson's place in Royal Mint Square, Stepney. One small room, in which the family (three children) did everything – relax, sleep, eat, cook, wash – except go to the toilet. This they shared with eleven other families. Or the room in Greenwich where a man, his wife and three kids lived. It was about seven feet by seven feet; a double bed took up most of the room, the rest was occupied by unpacked belongings stacked to the ceiling, leaving only about one and a half square yards of floor space. The family shared a kitchen and lavatory with six other families. Consider the rooms in Notting Hill where Maggie O'Shannon lived before she squatted; they were rather like the place I visited in Brockley: sewage came up through the floor every day, all day. Keeping the place clean was impossible. Complain to the landlord? He ignores you. Take him to court? That's equivalent to giving yourself notice to quit and, with a couple of kids, finding another hovel isn't going to be easy; that means ending up 'on the welfare' and no one wants that. Consider the place in Ilford (yes, nice respectable Ilford) where we discovered a family living in a damp, leaky place with no electricity. Or think what it means to have a room so damp that the wallpaper peels off as soon as you re-paper it. Another family I met once were so overcrowded that the husband used to sleep in the car. That was possible until he had a car crash: after that he had to move in with the rest.

Cheshire Street, Stepney, September 1969: one family occupy a room at the top of a warehouse; man, wife, two kids; the father has never been out of work. There is no electricity in the room, the light is rigged up through a crude lead from the warehouse below. This family have not even the luxury of sharing a toilet or water supply with two dozen other families. There is no running water or toilet on the premises. Water was obtained from a friend down the road; in the corner of the room was a plastic bucket, with a curtain to pull round it. The family used this as a toilet, and had to tip the contents down the drain outside the building after use. In another place in the same street, overrun with rats, lived another family who finally squatted in Arbour Square, Stepney in September 1969. Arbour Square is no palace, but at least you don't wake up to find rats in the children's bed.

Bronchitis, colds, skin diseases, sores, lung infections; no one has ever measured the illness or death caused by bad housing. 3,000,000 families live like this in Britain today, that makes about 9,500,000 people. There are empty office blocks, empty luxury flats with rents at £10 per week, and there are empty houses in every borough awaiting demolition in one, two, three, five or eight years' time.

You think you've seen everything; you think nothing can shock you anymore, but you soon discover you're wrong. I've spent five years looking round the slums, hostels and hovels of this country, and I've got a good imagination, but not in a hundred years could I have imagined anything like Glen Faba and Riverfields. In March 1970 I drove into Essex, through Harlow and into the quiet village of Roydon on the Essex–Hertfordshire border. A few miles from the village is an un-made road. If you travel down this, driving at about two miles per hour because of the ruts and boulders, you find yourself in forty acres of bush land. Tucked away in the bushes are tiny, dilapidated wooden sheds, many of them so broken down that no one would want them in their garden. And yet amazingly enough there are people living in them, somehow existing in this quiet part of Essex with the nearest electricity supply miles away, the nearest gas main miles away, the nearest water supply miles away and the nearest toilet miles away. If this is not bad enough, the inhabitants are all old people – with an average age of about sixty-five. They've been left there to rot for years. The first person I met was Dennis: he was fetching water to make his tea on a calor gas ring. His source of water? The nearby River Lea – muddy and murky but the only source available. Since 1966 these shanty towns have been the responsibility of the Epping and Ongar Rural District Council. The

Essex County Welfare Department are 'powerless' to help. This place is inhabited to this day, despite all the welfare and social service policies that are supposed to help those in need.

Is it getting any better? The answer is no, it is getting worse. Figures are fairly superfluous, but for anyone who wants them to prove that there's a housing crisis of the most enormous proportion in this country here are a few for consideration, in addition to those already mentioned:

November 1966: *Cathy Come Home* is first shown on television.

Number of people in Part III Accommodation is nearly 13,000.

November 1967: one year later, this has increased to 14,000.

November 1968: *Cathy Come Home* shown for the third time. Squatters campaign begins; the number of people in Part III Accommodation has risen to 15,574.

April 1969: the number is nearing 19,000.

1971: the number exceeds 21,000.

1966–8: figures for those three years show that the number of children in care in England and Wales because of homelessness or bad housing conditions varied little around the 5,000 mark. No improvement here.

November 1966: number of people on housing waiting lists in London is 150,000.

1967–9: an increase of 20,000 people on waiting lists in the London area.

London remains the worst city in Europe for housing. The Milner Holland committee on housing reported in 1965 and made comparisons between London and seven cities overseas. London was the worst: the others had better systems for regulating rents; security of tenure in them was more widely available.

The shortage of dwellings in London is estimated to be about 270,000. In addition to this there are 190,000 occupied dwellings unfit for human habitation. This situation is the worst it has ever been, and is getting worse every year.

The much publicized Greve Report proved officially what everyone concerned had known for years – that the housing situation in Britain is a national disaster and should be treated as such. No government, however, has been prepared to do this.

All this is the basic human reason why squatters occupy empty property and challenge the housing authorities.

2. The Birth of the Movement

The current squatters movement was born in 1968 but, like all new-born organisms, the seed had been sown long before. Recent events are the result of a long period of dormancy and germination during which the influence of past events has been at work. These influential events were the squatters movements following the First World War, the much larger squatting campaign following the Second World War and the various direct action campaigns which had taken place at the hostels and in the slums over the previous few years.

We need not pay too much attention to the 1919 campaign, it is now so long ago and was on such a small scale. It is enough to say that the 'homes fit for heroes' just did not exist; returning servicemen successfully seized empty properties to live in – to the astonishment and rage of the government of the day.

Thirty years later politicians were equally taken aback by a similar movement after the 1939–45 war. In the spring of 1945 empty houses in Blantyre, Scotland, were occupied. But it was the 'Vigilante movement' of the summer of that year that really shook the government into action. 'Vigilante' groups were committees made up largely of ex-servicemen who installed homeless families in empty properties by night. The movement started, and was at its strongest, in south coast resorts like Southend-on-Sea, Brighton and Hastings. The occupations were successful – legal action against the squatters was slow and difficult to institute as it often took some time to trace the absentee property owners.

The movement had begun as a protest against large houses in these resorts being left empty for most of the year in order that they might be let at very high rents during the holiday season. As the campaign grew it developed into an attack on the right of landlords to do as they wished with 'their' property, particularly if the exercise of these rights entailed leaving houses empty while other people were homeless. The growth of the movement ensured its success; the government was forced to give wider powers to local authorities to requisition empty property for housing purposes while the threat of further direct action compelled the councils to use these powers.

Despite all this, people were still homeless and, less than a year later, on 8 May 1946, Mr James Fielding, a cinema projectionist of Scunthorpe in Lincolnshire, moved with his family into the officers' mess of a disused anti-aircraft camp. When news of this got out he was quickly joined by other young couples. Other camps nearby were also occupied and homeless families seized several more in the Sheffield area. The two groups linked up to form themselves into the Squatters Protection Society. These ideas caught on rapidly and within a few months hundreds of camps all over Britain had been occupied by thousands of homeless families.

The authorities were extremely embarrassed by all this. They were faced on the one hand by an acute housing shortage while, on the other, with people literally out on the streets, they were in control of hundreds of empty service camps which they had no intention of using. The authorities immediately reacted by trying to pass the buck – each department tried to avoid having to face the situation and each disclaimed any responsibility for the squatters. The rapid and spontaneous growth of the movement made it impossible for the government to crush it; this, together with the obvious moral justification for the campaign and the authorities' complete inability to house people, meant that terms had to be made with the squatters. Local authorities were instructed to turn on water and electricity at the camps and to provide essential services. This in turn served to encourage more squatters, and by 11 October 1946 the government announced that there were 39,535 people squatting in 1,038 camps in England and Wales plus a further 4,000 squatters in Scotland.

Unable to stamp out or buy off the movement, the government tried to contain it by reasoning with it. They declared that they were confident that the squatters would 'see reason' and 'move out when the situation had been explained to them'. This approach too was doomed to failure. The only 'reason' that people could see was that while they had no homes and were being prosecuted for sleeping rough there were good properties lying empty. Houses, shops, disused schools, race tracks and hotels began to be occupied – the movement was turning to the cities as the camps became full. The climax of the movement was reached on the days succeeding 8 September, for on that day 148 luxury flats in the Duchess of Bedford buildings in Kensington were occupied and this seizure was followed by the occupation of flats and hotels in Marylebone, Holland Park, Camden Hill, Victoria, Regents Park, Blooms-bury and other key places. This really frightened the Labour administration; the government's fear for itself overcame its sympathy with the homeless. Occupation of army camps and seaside houses had been bad enough but tolerable, the seizure of property in other cities while more ominous was still acceptable, but for the squatters to move into the capital was just too much. Why, they might even attempt an occupation of Parliament next – and that would have prevented the discussion of the housing shortage. On 10 September the police were instructed to keep watch on all unoccupied property in order to prevent further squatting. Certain buildings occupied by squatters were cordoned off, among them Abbey Lodge, a block of flats in Regents Park, and the Ivanhoe Hotel, a 600-room building in Bloomsbury. The Home Office instructed Scotland Yard to 'enquire into the origins of the organization behind the squatters'.

Cordoning off buildings resulted in street demonstrations, including a 'lie down' in the road outside Abbey Lodge which held up traffic for half an hour. Similar scenes developed at the Ivanhoe. These demonstrations produced some results and certain amounts of food and blankets were allowed into the besieged buildings. Later in the week mounted police were used to disperse demonstrators and there were even rumours that tear gas would be used – these, however, proved to be unfounded. It was clear that a highly inflammable situation was developing and it was at this point that the government used its ultimate weapon. On Saturday 14 September five com-

munists were arrested for organizing the occupation of the
Duchess of Bedford buildings and were charged with two very
strange offences: conspiracy to commit trespass and forcible
entry. The second of these charges comes under the Forcible
Entry Act of 1381 and I will discuss both more fully, later in
this book. Communists had become involved in the squatting
movement quite late; indeed, at first they had been quite cool
towards it and had even denounced the Vigilante campaign of
the previous year. It was only in London that they were really
active – and even there it was certainly not the communists
who inspired the movement despite the impression given by
part of the press and fostered by the CP itself.[1] A study of the
Abbey Lodge squatters (Pilot Papers, November 1946, by
Diana Murray Hill) revealed this quite clearly. The Communist Party had, however, involved itself in the organization
of some occupations in London and the government was able
to use this to victimize five of its members as a means of
deterring other squatters.

Certainly this clamp-down by the government effectively
halted the squatting campaign in London – particularly the
spectacular 'squats' in large buildings. This should not be
allowed, however, to detract from the overwhelming success of
the movement. The Ministry of Works, which earlier in the
year had declared itself not interested in the question, now
handed over 850 former service camps to the squatters who
were thus entirely successful in obtaining homes. In London
many of the squatters were given alternative accommodation
by the authorities and the government was compelled to face
the housing crisis. The movement was almost completely
successful and this success cannot be concealed by the arrest of
five communists.

The spirit and success of the 1945–6 squatting campaigns
made them an important influence on those people who initiated the present campaign. It was during a series of largely
successful actions in hostels and slums that the idea of squatting was revived. The first and best known of these was the

1. I must make it clear that my remarks are not directed towards the
many party members who, as individuals, sincerely assisted in the early
stages of the campaign, but to the official Communist Party line.

long battle against the Kent County Council over the inhuman rules in force at their King Hill Hostel at West Malling. This action began in August 1965 and went on until July 1966. Apart from generally poor conditions in the hostel, there were two rules which were particular sources of complaint: the one against husbands living in and the other which decreed that after three months even the women and children were turned out, whether they had found alternative accommodation or not.

In that August of 1965 Mrs Joan Daniels was due to be evicted as her three months had expired. On this occasion, however, the welfare officials received an unpleasant shock – instead of Joan and her family moving out, her husband, Stan, moved in. Welfare officials then cut off the water supply but the solidarity shown by the other residents enabled the Daniels successfully to resist attempts to evict them. Stan and Joan Daniels' action was the flash-point – thirteen other husbands moved in and the King Hill campaign had begun. Throughout the next eleven months the homeless families, together with a small group of direct actionists known as the 'Friends of King Hill', waged a bitter and militant struggle against the Kent County Council. The no-husband rule was ignored and so too was the three-month-limit rule. The demands of the campaigners were simple – the official repeal of the two inhuman rules and the improvement of conditions in the hostel.

The councillors of the Kent County Council did everything in their power to defeat the campaign.[1] Smear tactics were produced; threats were offered; the 'we won't help you until you behave yourselves' line was tried – and they all failed. In fact every bluster and every move from the council merely served to increase the determination of the families and caused more husbands to move in. The council then went to the courts and obtained injunctions restraining certain husbands from living with their families. On two occasions *men were actually jailed* for ignoring these, and each time, on their release, the husbands went straight back to their families in the hostel.

While all this was going on the families and the 'Friends of

1. With one exception – Councillor Kenneth Josephs, Tory member for Ramsgate.

King Hill' continued their campaign. When persuasion failed they adopted other tactics. Dr A. Elliot, the chief Welfare Officer, was embarrassed to discover pickets outside his house on Christmas Day 1965. Marches were made to his house and leaflets were distributed to his neighbours describing exactly what he was doing to the people living in King Hill. Other marches and picketings were held outside both County Hall and Brixton Prison while the husbands were in jail. Kent County Council enjoyed what must have been the worst press publicity ever endured by a local council – a record to be broken later only by Redbridge.

After nearly a year the Kent County Council finally backed down – in July 1966 they accepted what was really a *fait accompli*. The husbands who had been living with their families for the past few months were now 'allowed' to stay, the three-month limit was ended, conditions were considerably improved and control of King Hill Hostel was taken out of the hands of Dr Elliot and given to the Children's Department. As the *Observer* later remarked, the campaign had achieved in twelve months what twelve years of governmental admonishment to the Kent County Council had failed to achieve. It was a victory for direct action.

Following this victory other direct action struggles began, all equally successful. Abridge Hostel in Essex, which I have already described in the first chapter, was closed down after a battle lasting three months and all the families living in it were rehoused. Here again the campaign was started by the husbands who, with the assistance of a small band of direct actionists, broke the rules and visited their families out of hours. The high point of this campaign came when we occupied the hostel armed with tools and materials in order to convert the dormitory into separate family units. Efforts by the police to remove us proved unsuccessful, for as soon as we were carried out we climbed in again through the windows. A telephone call to Mr W. Boyce, the Essex County Welfare Officer, resulted in his promise of immediate action – we gave him one week 'or else we will return with one hundred people'. Three days later the Welfare Committee announced the closure of the hostel and the families were rehoused. This, despite the fact that the county council had claimed earlier that, unfortunately, they were only a welfare authority and not a housing authority and so could not rehouse people.

It was during the Abridge struggle that one of the husbands, Alf Williams, mentioned the possibility of squatting. We decided that if all else failed some empty houses in Essex would be occupied to enable these families to live together. Our speedy victory rendered this course unnecessary but the idea had been planted and it lived on.

About a year later, towards the end of 1967, Wandsworth Borough Council in south-west London tried to impose a nine-month limit to the stay of families in the council's temporary accommodation. Alderman Jack Parker, chairman of the Welfare Committee, described it as 'a genuine social experiment'. To the families of Durham Buildings in Battersea it was more of a genuine social threat. A campaign was mounted to bring this rule to an end and similar methods to those already described were employed again. There were demonstrations in the council chamber, a march on Alderman Parker's house and a march on the Kentish Town home of Kenneth Robinson (the governmental minister responsible at the time). This short campaign was also successful and promises were obtained from the council that the rule would be rescinded. A letter was also received from Kenneth Robinson stating that no families would be put 'on the streets so that a need to take children into care would not arise'.[1]

It is interesting to recall that a number of Wandsworth councillors claimed that they had never intended that the rule should be adhered to and had meant it only as a threat to be used to 'encourage' the families to look for alternative accommodation. Whether or not this is true we shall never know, but quite apart from the virtual impossibility of working-class families with children finding accommodation, one cannot help wondering if the members of the Wandsworth Borough Council really believe that these threats could in any way be called 'welfare'. It was at this point in the history of the movement that we considered the possibility of pushing the campaign a step further and actually engaging in the business of

1. Dated 10 November 1967.

struggling for the rehousing of homeless families. Squatting was again discussed and, as the Liberal Party was at the time campaigning for the re-letting of empty property in the Home Road district of Battersea, an obvious target presented itself. However, for a number of different reasons at the time nothing further happened.

Then in the summer of 1968 I was involved in another campaign, this time at Coventry Cross, a GLC slum in Bromley-by-Bow in the East End of London. After discussions and some meetings the tenants formed the Coventry Cross Action Committee to protest against the appalling conditions – rats, extreme overcrowding, faulty drainage, baths in the kitchens – and to demand rehousing. Once again the question of squatting was raised and empty houses in Dagenham were suggested; this time the plan may well have gone ahead had we not won the struggle so quickly. Once more we mounted marches and pickets and this time there were two television programmes describing conditions on the estate. We took forty East End children to the house of Horace Cutler, chairman of the GLC Housing Committee, and it was a splendid sight to see them let loose on his Buckinghamshire lawn. When we took the same army and unleashed it upon the offices of the Tower Hamlets Public Health Department the results were equally amusing. We also asked Mr George Vale, the Eastern District Housing Officer of the GLC, to act and his refusal to co-operate forced the tenants to visit him at his home in Gidea Park and to discuss the matter with him on the telephone. It was rumoured that at one point the complaints were so frequent that his telephone was in constant use. A weekend 'camp-out' was planned to take place on the lawn of the GLC Director of Housing, Mr J. P. Macey, at his house at Merrow, Guildford. However, at the beginning of September the GLC announced the closure of Coventry Cross for modernization and began the rehousing of the 190 families living there, so all our further plans were no longer needed.

What we had learned from all our campaigns was that direct action worked where individual complaints failed. The time had obviously come for us to take the struggle a stage further and to campaign, not only for better conditions and for the abolition of inhuman rules in temporary accommodation, but actually to occupy empty property and so directly to challenge the housing policies of the local authorities. A squatting campaign was clearly on the cards; it only needed a spark to set it off.

On 13 November 1968, almost exactly two years after its first showing, *Cathy Come Home* was repeated on television for the second time. A friend of mine who had never seen the play before was upset and shocked by it; as we talked I tried to explain to her that 'upset and shock' were not enough. The first showing had stirred people; everyone, but everyone, suddenly cared for the homeless, and to prove it they gave a few pounds to Shelter, a charity formed during the outcry following the showing of the film. Housing had been part of every politician's platform, particularly at election time. They had always cared and for years they had promised action, but with *Cathy* they all became even more 'concerned' in their speeches and made even more promises. Politicians of all parties fell over themselves and each other in the rush to express their interest in the problem of homelessness.

All this 'interest' and 'concern' was produced by *Cathy Come Home* and the public pressure that followed it – Shelter kept up the pressure by continually bringing the subject home to people, not allowing them to forget it again. No one can deny that their publicity has been very effective and hard-hitting. They have criticized the official figures for homelessness, arguing that a homeless family is not just a family living in a hostel but also any family living in accommodation so poor or overcrowded as to make decent family life impossible. The term 'homeless family', maintained Shelter, must be redefined along these lines.[1] As a result of their pressure Shelter have raised money, a great deal of money – over £3 million to date. By using this money to finance housing associations and by obtaining additional grants from local authorities, it has rehoused, on average, six families a day. This is a considerable achievement due to the sincere and hard-working people who make up the organization. It is clear that no one working

1. See the excellent pamphlet published by Shelter, *Face the Facts.*

in the field of housing campaigns can afford to ignore Shelter
or totally dismiss its work.

I must stress that any criticism I may make of Shelter is
made with this acknowledgement in mind. What I have to say
should not be seen as a condemnation of either the organization or of the people who work in it, but rather as a critique of
the idea that their programme contains the answer to the housing problem. I consider that we need a more militant approach
and effort in order to tackle the situation. I don't want to give
the impression that I think their work futile. I make this point
because I have no wish to stir up a row between the squatters
and Shelter. Both organizations are united in their criticism of,
and attack on, the authorities' housing policies, and in putting
the case for direct action I do not mean to undermine the
value of Shelter's work.

That being said I want now to point out the limitations
placed on the work of Shelter or of any other charity. One is
to be seen in the fact that, in obtaining grants from local
authorities for housing associations, Shelter is to a great extent
governed by the dictates of that authority. Most authorities insist on the right to nominate the families to be helped, with the
result that they give the housing associations those families
they would have to rehouse anyway; families affected by clearance orders, redevelopment schemes and so on. In this way
the charities, by doing the job that the authorities have a
statutory obligation to carry out, are assisting them in their
failure to provide enough houses. The final result of this is that
the charities are then unable to help those families for which
they were formed – the really desperate homeless. Shelter's
former director, Des Wilson, was very aware of this limitation
on his work and campaigns vigorously against the nomination
practice. However, because charities work within the system
and are dependent upon it for co-operation, they are tied no
matter how much they may dislike the idea.

My main reason for opting for direct action rather than for
the 'charity' approach is that, despite everything that the
charities do, the problem is actually getting worse. Seeing this
is of prime importance and, unfortunate as it may be, not even
Shelter would want to deny it. By the end of 1968 local

authority housing lists in London alone increased from 100,000 to 160,000; the current figure is 170,000.

The plain fact is that direct action is now the only answer left, for everything else has been tried. Politicians have 'cared' about the housing crisis for years but successive governments have not stopped it from getting worse – and neither has Shelter. It is clear then that only a radical change in the priorities of our society can solve the problem, and it is equally clear that no government has shown itself prepared to make this radical change no matter what criticism and public censure is heaped upon it. This so-obvious fact hit me as I talked to my friend on the night of the third showing of *Cathy*: 'But remember,' I said to her, 'you can cry all you like about Cathy, but things won't change until people act.' And that, in a nutshell, was it.

Mass action by ordinary people – the millions who suffer from the housing shortage – was not only something that I advocated as a revolutionary tactic, but something which had become the only way these people could hope to get decent homes. The governments have listened to nothing – they must be made to listen and to change their priorities or to get out. We had seen how direct action could succeed in small ways; we had now to push it a step further. After all we could go from hostel to hostel for the next five years and get involved in successful campaigns without coming near to solving the root problems of housing and without succeeding in drastically shaking the authorities. What was needed was an all-out attack on the authorities by ordinary people taking action by themselves. But how could this be started? What could we, a small group of activists, do? The influences of the past movements, of the actions in the hostels and the way in which squatting had continuously cropped up during our earlier discussions and, most of all, because squatting was an action which would actually house desperate families, made it seem the best way to start such a movement.

All this went through my mind on that evening of the third showing of *Cathy*. By three o'clock in the morning I had become convinced that a new squatters campaign was both necessary and realistic. I woke up some friends who were staying in my house, they too were enthusiastic and we immediately began to discuss ways and means to initiate the campaign. On 14 November 1968 the London Squatters Campaign came into being.

3. Learning the Game

So, early in the morning of 14 November, two friends and I decided to put the idea of squatting into practice. Clearly the first priority was to involve a small group of people who could be trusted. Trust was the all-important factor, for if the first demonstration flopped it would be a great setback to the new campaign. I contacted people whom I knew to be active and interested in the housing field, and on Monday 18 November about fifteen people assembled in my house to discuss the idea. They came from all over London, from Essex, from Kent, and from Surrey. It would perhaps be interesting to comment on the composition of this group. Most were from the revolutionary libertarian left – there were a couple of anarchists, and three or four people from the Solidarity group, and some 'unattached' libertarians, like Jim Radford. There were also two young Liberals, John and Mary Dixon, who came all the way from Camberley, and there were a few more non-political people. All were united by their interest in housing, and most had been involved in housing struggles in the past, including those already described in Chapter 2.

The idea of a new squatters campaign was met with enthusiasm and it was agreed to hold a demonstration as soon as possible. There was some discussion as to what we should call our group. We wanted a name that at the right time would attract immediate press interest, for we would be dependent on press coverage to get the campaign publicized. 'London Squatters' was easy to arrive at, but we finally had to settle for London Squatters Campaign, although we would have liked the last word to begin with a 'D' thus giving us the initials LSD.

There was then some discussion about the aims of the campaign. No actual statement was written out, but I think it would be correct to say that they centred around four points.

The immediate aim was, of course, simply the rehousing of families from hostels or slums by means of squatting. However, most people present also spoke of wider aims, and it is important that these are understood. All the people there were convinced that direct action was both justifiable and necessary, but everyone realized that we could make only limited gains unless our influence spread. The three wider aims of the campaign were therefore concerned with spreading our influence.

Obviously we hoped that our action would spark off a squatting campaign on a mass scale, and that homeless people and slum dwellers would be inspired to squat in large numbers by small but successful actions. But the main purpose of the movement was even wider than this – we hoped to start an all-out attack on the housing authorities, with ordinary people taking action for themselves. Finally, and closely in conjunction with this, we saw our campaign as having a radicalizing effect on existing movements in the housing field – tenants associations, action committees, community project groups, etc. If these could be radicalized and linked together then we would really have achieved something.

It is important that these wider aims be understood because many people feel that the squatters, even if they succeeded in launching a mass campaign, can do little more than Shelter to solve the housing problem. Squatting, after all, is only concerned with existing empty property. But this is to miss the point. Squatting should be the movement of ordinary people to challenge the authorities on the whole issue. It must become the living demonstration that ordinary people will no longer accept the intolerable housing shortage. It must become the threat that will compel government, national and local, to change its priorities.

A further discussion on how to launch the campaign followed our first meeting. It was decided that we should initially hold a token squat, both to publicize the movement and to serve as a trial run for ourselves. We fully realized that moving in families was a great responsibility, so we delayed until we felt more able to embark on it.

We also discussed where we should hold our first demonstration. One person, Trevor Jackles, had already begun drawing up a list of some empty offices and flats in the East End. He was asked to carry on with this work. I was asked to continue my investigation into all the legal ramifications of squatting. A further meeting was arranged for 25 November.

On that day all our plans were finalized. By now a few more people had been brought in, including some people from the International Socialist group. Our 'property researcher' had done his work and we decided that the first demonstration should take place on the following Sunday, 1 December, at the Hollies, a large block of luxury flats next to Snaresbrook station, in Wanstead. They had been built four years previously and many were still empty because of the high prices being asked – anything up to £15,000. Quite obviously these flats were not going to help solve the problem of working-class families living in slums or hostels. Luxury flats lying empty for years while people rot in slums is an apt symbol of the false priorities of our 'affluent' society. So the Hollies was an excellent first target. Two o'clock Sunday 1 December was the time set for our first action. All present agreed only to tell friends who could be trusted, and these were to be instructed to meet at Snaresbrook station at 1.45 p.m. Banners and posters were made and our 'property researcher' visited the Companies Registry and obtained useful information about the owner of the Hollies which he used in the leaflet we produced.

But before the demonstration we looked carefully into the legal charges that could be levelled against us. We did not seriously expect them to be used, but we felt that we should examine all the legal ramifications of the campaign we were starting. This was to be of immense value to us later, in particular at Redbridge when we presented an almost insoluble problem to the council and police who, try as they might, could not find an offence to charge us with. Time and time again the councillors and officials bemoaned this fact. In addition to this it was also important for us to avoid breaking the law in order to involve homeless families in the campaign. After all, we thought that if we could say to families that squatting was only civil trespass and not an offence for which they could be prosecuted, then we were far more likely to be able to involve them in squatting activities.

What then were the possible charges we had to avoid? The most obvious was 'breaking and entering'. Naturally we did not want to break into the premises, but the term 'breaking' in this context is so wide as to include even opening a door, and we would certainly have to do this. However, breaking and entering is not itself a charge in English law, but is a constituent part of the offence of housebreaking, and this must have an 'intent' – to commit a crime, usually larceny. We obviously had no such intent, so this charge would clearly not apply. (The 1968 Theft Act did not alter this principle.) 'Malicious damage' was another possibility, but there was little to worry about on this score as we had no intention of doing any damage. We were out to demonstrate, not to wreck the place.

There were, however, a number of serious charges that we thought of as possibilities, although we considered it extremely unlikely that any of them would be used as they would need the consent of the Director of Public Prosecutions. We just could not envisage him instituting proceedings which would mean an Old Bailey trial following our relatively minor demonstration at a block of flats in Snaresbrook. Nevertheless, we took these charges into account, as much for future action as for the Hollies demonstration itself.

The first possibility was 'forcible entry', under the statute of 1381 – the same charge the organizers of the occupation of the Duchess of Bedford Buildings had been convicted of in 1946. Briefly this makes it an offence to enter into land or tenements 'with strong hand or multitude of people'. Avoiding this charge was relatively simple for two reasons. First, we had no intention of using force, we preferred to enter by means of a trick and this does not constitute a forcible entry. Second, there would be no entry in the terms of the statute. Entry under the Forcible Entry Act means entry with intent to claim and remain in possession, rather than entry with the mere intent to trespass for a few hours. So this charge would clearly not apply to token demonstrations, although we realized it could well apply to real occupation of property with homeless families, and would thus have to be kept in mind on future occasions.

Two other possible charges were 'riotous assembly' and 'unlawful assembly'. Riot was easy to avoid as one of the constituents is that the offenders must be prepared to use force or violence against any persons who may oppose them in the execution of their common purpose. We agreed therefore that if anyone opposed us we would not assist each other and, if one of us was being obstructed, the rest of the demonstrators would ignore this and walk round the obstruction. So we ruled out the chance of riot charges. Unlawful assembly is a much wider charge, but was also not too hard to avoid. Briefly it is an assembly which leads or seems likely to lead to a breach of the peace. We agreed then that we must avoid this possibility by behaving in an orderly fashion at all times and refrain from charging wildly about or causing a public disturbance.

What, finally, of trespass? Clearly our action would be a trespass. Trespass, however, is a civil wrong, and not a criminal offence. Trespassers cannot be prosecuted, they can only be sued in the civil court by the owner of the land, and we just could not see the property company that owned the Hollies doing that. But what of conspiracy to trespass, that strange 'offence' that the five communists had been convicted of in 1946, and with which the Greek Embassy demonstrators had been charged, but which had been dropped when they all pleaded guilty to unlawful assembly? Could we avoid this charge? The answer to that was no — quite clearly we were conspiring to trespass on the Hollies, and indeed any squat may well involve a like conspiracy. What then would our defence against this charge be? Without going into the history of the law of conspiracy, let me simply say that our defence would be that the 'offence' of conspiracy to commit trespass is not an offence known to English law, and has never been held to be one in the courts. It is true that the 1946 squatters were charged with it and convicted, but this is not of real legal authority as the matter was never taken to appeal. It is the decisions of the appeal courts that form important legal precedents, and conspiracy to commit trespass has never been held to be an offence in these. This charge, therefore, did not worry us unduly.

We decided to occupy the roof of the building for about four

hours. As the outer door to the flats was locked we appointed
two people to look into the best way of obtaining access. The
press had to be informed; two more people with previous experience and whom reporters knew and respected took on this
job. It was arranged that for the sake of security the press
would be met at Stratford underground station at 1.30 p.m.
and be told where to go. By the time they arrived at Snaresbrook we calculated that the entry party would be ready to
go in. The plans were then carefully laid and everything was
prepared for the Sunday.

The two appointed to discover the best means of entry had
decided that deception was necessary, so Alf Williams and
another of those assembled walked up to the outer door of the
flats carrying tool bags resembling those used by workers of the
London Electricity Board and rang the bell. They had no
trouble in gaining access 'to inspect the wiring'. A few minutes
later, as numerous reporters and television crews arrived, the
main party made its way up to the outer door. The plan was,
of course, that the 'electricians' already inside would open it
and let us all in. To our horror, however, the porter opened the
door, but he was too surprised to see us all there to realize
what was about to happen. Instead of closing the door immediately, which would have presented us with quite a problem (although not an insurmountable one, as we still had our
two 'electricians' inside to open it), he came out to demand
what we wanted. While I tried to speak to him, the rest of the
party stepped behind him and into the Hollies – I followed. We
rushed up the numerous flights of stairs and finally reached the
top. Carefully removing some bars from a window in order not
to damage anything, we climbed out onto the sun roof, unfurled our banner and showered leaflets down into the street
below, where some of our number had remained and were
already giving out leaflets. It was 2.03 p.m., everything had
gone well, despite the porter coming to the door. We even
discovered that some of the press had followed us out onto the
roof. As we looked down we could see small groups of people
gathering and apparently discussing the situation. Members of
our group were giving out leaflets and we could see that they
were being read. The neighbourhood became quite a hive of

activity. Meanwhile the porter had called the police and a couple of constables arrived and told us we would be arrested if we did not leave immediately. When we asked what for they did not reply. A senior policeman arrived and told us to leave and again we refused. The police were powerless: we were committing no offence and, furthermore, unless the owner requested them to do so they could not even remove us. So Mr Joseph Kasner, head of the firm that built the Hollies, was sent for. He arrived and came out onto the roof to ask us to leave. Again we refused to do so and assured him that we would not do any damage. A brief conversation between Mr Kasner and the police resulted in their deciding to leave us there. In fact they had little choice – the only way to get us off would have been either to throw us over the balcony or somehow carry twenty of us through the window we had used.

We had intended to stay on the roof for four hours, but at 3.30 p.m. it seemed that we had made our point, so we held a short meeting on the roof and decided to come down and talk to the press and television reporters waiting in the street below. We also decided that we could jump into cars and vans and make for nearby Embassy Court, another block of largely empty luxury flats about a mile away and under the same ownership. So we went down and into the forecourt of the Hollies, where we were besieged by pressmen. We warned them that this was only the beginning and that in the future we would be occupying empty property with the intention of installing homeless families. Then we hurried off to Embassy Court followed by an entourage of journalists and onlookers including about a dozen teenagers from a local grammar school. The police arrived before us and prevented us from gaining entry, so we held a public meeting outside, where a number of people spoke about housing. One of our speakers, Alf Williams, carried a banner proclaiming, 'I lived in hostels for four years while these flats were empty.' It was Alf who had suggested squatting when involved at Abridge. He now lived in a council house in Harlow, but was still concerned with the plight of the homeless and he believed that direct action was necessary.

The speeches over, we all left Embassy Court and drifted off to our respective homes. The demonstration itself had been extremely successful. We now waited to see if it would have the desired effect – the production of publicity and public interest. As this was a new kind of activity we were fairly optimistic, but never in our wildest dreams did we anticipate the amount of coverage we received in the next few days. On the day following the demonstration my telephone did not stop ringing – in all I must have received something like 250 calls – and for the rest of the week the daily number remained extremely high. One of our number even recorded an interview for Canadian Radio; already we were international news!

The interest and the probing paid off – figures began to emerge on the amount of empty property. The *Guardian* on 3 December quoted from the 1966 sample census. According to this there were 470,000 empty dwellings in England and Wales and a further 30,000 in Scotland, making half a million in all. Another article, in *The Financial Times*, 12 December, stated that the G LC had 5,000 empty houses that they did not intend to use again.

Nearly all the publicity was sympathetic and at least a dozen pressmen asked to come to our next meeting. The first leader to appear on the subject of empty property appeared on 4 December in the *Guardian*. Strangely, the only criticism came from Des Wilson of Shelter. He agreed that we had done a good job in highlighting the issue, but warned that 'more direct action could do more harm than good because it could cause anger against the homeless population'.[1] At one point it seemed as though a serious rift might develop between Shelter and the squatters. However, this did not materialize because Des Wilson did not continue his attack, and we did not retaliate; instead both organizations declared that they were using different methods to fight the same problem.

The question for us now, of course, was what next? A success is far harder to follow than a failure. Our meeting of 3 December was packed out – nearly fifty people crammed into my front room. The new arrivals in the campaign included many people from Shelter and from the Young Liberals. It was

1. *Evening News,* 3 December 1968.

decided that our next demonstration should be just before Christmas and that we should try to get some homeless people to participate in it. We decided, however, that it would only be another token demonstration, as it would be unfair to squat a family so near Christmas. Again a couple of people were delegated to look into possible targets. The meeting also decided that we should, on the following two Sundays, undertake to canvass hostels and slums in the East End of London.

The next couple of weeks saw us visiting families in the East End and talking to them about our campaign. The reception we received was heartening; the vast majority were sympathetic. Few of them, however, were willing to squat, as most of them were frightened of breaking the law and of 'spoiling their chances' of getting a house, although most of them also fully realized that they had no such chance for the next five years at least. At that stage they had insufficient confidence in themselves or the strength of any movement to risk so drastic an action as squatting. Not everyone felt this reluctance, but many did. The canvassing was very worthwhile, however, not only because we were heartened by the favourable reception, but also because it made people think about action. In addition to the canvassing, I was personally in contact with some homeless families who lived in Council Buildings, a hostel in Poplar: they too were delighted to hear about the squatting campaign.

A number of meetings were held at my house to arrange our new squat. The two of us delegated to look around for empty properties had found an excellent target – a vicarage in Capworth Street, Leyton, that had been empty for at least three years. The existence of this place was nothing new to me, as two years earlier I had lived even nearer to it than I do now. Indeed, following our victorious struggle at Abridge Hostel, the Essex County Council had approached the small group of direct activists involved and asked us to help them with their homeless problem, by providing them with property to use for families. This, of course, was certainly not our role at all and anyway was quite beyond the capacity of the small group of people involved. However, this same vicarage had been empty then and we had approached the church authorities with a request that it be used for homeless families. This request was rejected without even being considered.

So this large old house, All Saints Old Vicarage, made an excellent target and an apt one, with Christmas so near. As with the Hollies, we 'cased the joint' well. The two of us who did this discovered that although the ground floor was properly secured and locked up, there was an easily accessible upstairs window that had been left unlocked. We used this on three or four occasions to enter the house and draw up plans. We decided that it would be possible to occupy the whole house and fairly effectively barricade ourselves in without doing any damage.

The demonstration was scheduled for the weekend of 21 and 22 December and we decided to make it a twenty-four hour stay-in. As with the Hollies elaborate security arrangements were drawn up. The press were to be met at 1.30 p.m. on 21 December at Holborn Station, supporters were to meet at 1.45 p.m. at Stratford Station, while the two dozen people in the 'entry party', which included some homeless people from Council Buildings, were to meet at a private house nearby at 12.30 p.m. Meanwhile one member of the group was to enter the house very early in the morning, while it was still dark, in order to let the 'entry party' in when it arrived. In order to make doubly sure of success we even planned an alternative target in case our plan to occupy the Old Vicarage leaked out.

On Saturday 21 December 1968 the plan was put into operation. At 6 a.m. Trevor Jackles climbed into the Old Vicarage through the usual window; at 10 a.m. I went to collect the families from Council Buildings in my van, which was already well loaded up with bedding and supplies; at 12.30 p.m. the 'entry party' met and, after a final briefing, made its way towards the target.

Unfortunately two things went wrong, both of which were certainly not our fault as they could not possibly have been foreseen. First, when the 'entry party' arrived they found the caretaker in the house. Somewhat taken aback he attacked one of our members, but then ran out to get help. This of course gave the squatters the opportunity they needed to secure themselves inside the house. Second, as I was driving my van up to the Old Vicarage, loaded up with supplies and three homeless people from Council Buildings, the gear box went! The van stopped, we were stranded.

I was frantic; I rushed up to two people in the street, offering them any amount of money if they could engage my gears and make the van go. Both were unsuccessful, but just as I was despairing a taxi drove by and I waved it down. The driver cannot possibly have known what he was letting himself in for, but he did not grumble. In about three minutes flat his taxi was full of mattresses, sleeping bags, oil heaters, stoves, banners, food and even a few people. He accepted it all without protest. The squatters campaign is deeply indebted to that taxi driver.

When we arrived at the Old Vicarage we found the place surrounded by police. Our goods were dragged out of the taxi onto the pavement and some money was thrown in the driver's direction. The police had not had time to arrange their cordon properly, and three of us rushed towards an open window. Somehow we got through it; either by climbing or by being dragged in by the squatters already inside. I rushed upstairs and grabbed hold of our megaphone and started shouting out of the window. Occupants of the flats opposite came out and listened as I harangued them. 'Is there any room at this inn for these homeless people?' I yelled, and 'Will the church deny families a home, one thousand nine hundred and sixty eight years after another family could not find accommodation?'

Meanwhile, the police decided to try and remove us and, although they managed to gain entry to the house, our barricades held in two rooms upstairs. It was a near thing though. By now our supporters and the press were arriving. As at the Hollies, leaflets were distributed and meetings held outside. At one point when more police arrived two people were arrested for obstruction, following a scuffle in the road. Those of us inside, however, had a problem. Owing to the mishaps that had occurred we had been unable to bring all our supplies in with us, so hurried had our entrance been. Many, after being dragged out of the taxi, had been left on the pavement. Some of the supporters down in the road proceeded thereafter to throw things up for us to catch at the windows. This went on for half an hour or more when a policeman suddenly arrested Jim Radford for assault, claiming that a bundle of blankets which Jim had thrown had hit him on the head. This provoked a brief incident and another man, Bryan Symons, was arrested. These arrests however only deterred the throwers for a short while, and soon we, upstairs, were receiving more supplies. Later still some policemen even started to hand things up to us. The arrests resulted in Bryan Symons being found guilty on one minor charge. Originally he had been charged on four counts. The two charges against Jim Radford of assault and obstruction were dismissed completely.

The demonstration was a success – we stayed inside for twenty-four hours as we had said we would. The amount of press publicity was far smaller than for the Hollies, and much less than we had hoped for. From this angle the occupation of the Old Vicarage was something of a disappointment. Only a couple of the newspapers on Sunday 22 December carried stories and on Monday 23 December we received only a few paragraphs' coverage. However, the twenty-four hours stay-in was invaluable practice for us. The demonstration taught us a great deal about how to organize a real occupation where we might be under siege for some time. So although the publicity was rather disappointing, the demonstration certainly had its uses.

Before ending this account of our second action I must pay particular tribute to one of the women from Council Buildings. Margaret Beresford, who will feature largely in this book later on, had been unable to gain access to the house. This had its value – she was able to talk to the press outside and tell them about Council Buildings. It must have been tiring for Margaret but she steadfastly refused to go home. 'I've come on this demonstration and I'll stay to the end,' she declared. And she did. Margaret Beresford, a middle-aged woman, spent twenty-four hours outside the Old Vicarage, and nothing we said could persuade her to go back to Council Buildings before the demonstration was over.

The usefulness of token demonstrations was now over. The time had now come for what we all regarded as 'the crunch' – the actual installing of homeless families in empty property.

4. Redbridge

Our next move was vital. We had carefully drawn up detailed plans, both for the Hollies demonstration and the Old Vicarage squat, but we realized that we would have to be ten times more careful and have everything organized down to the last detail. We knew that in moving families we were taking on a great responsibility, as this actually involved moving people's homes. We decided therefore that we should spend several weeks in preparation.

We held numerous planning meetings throughout January 1969, both at my house and at the Roti, an Indian restaurant in Walthamstow High Street. The news that we intended to move families into empty property drew in an even wider group of people than before.

A number of committees were set up to arrange particular aspects of the squat. There was a Workman's Committee whose job it was to 'case' the houses and ensure that we could lay on the essential services, and also to estimate what barricades we needed. There was the Supply and Transport Committee whose job it was to gather supplies of both food and furniture and lay on transport and, finally, there was the Planning and Co-ordinating Committee whose job it was to arrange all the details of time, date, place, etc.

The first thing to do was to decide on the location. Several places were considered. A return to the Old Vicarage was even suggested, but we decided that we should occupy local council property as it is the councils who statutorily ought to be housing people and we considered that we would get more public sympathy if we attacked them for leaving houses empty. Further, we reckoned that any local council would be very embarrassed by all the publicity of a sustained campaign against them. We knew that it was this kind of publicity that we needed, because we fully understood that we were few in number and that if the authorities wanted ruthlessly to smash us they could. Our only defence against this was to avoid such a confrontation by obtaining the kind of publicity which would make it difficult for the authorities to do this.

A local council was thus the agreed 'victim' and the discussion then centred on which council. Redbridge and Newham were 'short-listed'. The arguments in favour of Redbridge were that the council embarked upon its central Ilford redevelopment plan and was thus leaving a considerable number of houses empty. Furthermore, there was considerable local feeling about this – the Ilford Town Centre Residents Association was opposed both to the boarding up of houses and to the whole redevelopment plan and the small Labour group on the council was also in favour of letting the empty houses. Both groups had already been campaigning along these lines for some considerable time. From the point of view of 'local feeling' Redbridge was ideal, as all the usual 'constitutional' methods of getting the houses used had been exhausted: direct action was, literally, the only thing left.

Alternatively, there were arguments against Redbridge; it was a very middle-class borough, and we did not know just how this would affect things. True, there was local opposition to the council, but would this extend to support of the squatters? The London Borough of Newham was just the opposite however – a very working-class borough with an appalling housing problem. As we wanted to arouse those in bad housing Newham also presented a good target, although the policy of its council over empty houses was nothing like as bad as in Redbridge. Nevertheless, there were empty houses in Newham, so serious consideration was also given to these.

Our Workman's Committee therefore agreed to look over houses in both Redbridge and Newham. Early in January 1969 they entered a number of 'selected residences' in Oakfield Road, Ilford, and in Hatfield Road, Maryland. They reported back that the Hatfield Road houses were in poor condition, so that ruled out Newham as our target. The Redbridge houses, on the other hand, were in excellent condition with water and electricity services which our tradesmen could easily 'lay on'

with only a little work. Further research into the Ilford redevelopment scheme revealed that it had not even been approved
by the Ministry of Housing and anyway was not due to start
for some years — and yet there were houses deliberately being
left to rot (some for nearly ten years). Redbridge became our
target.

There was now a great deal of work to be done in organizing
the squat and planning our tactics. We decided to organize a
public march on 9 February to meet at Manor Park Station. As
this was in the London Borough of Newham we thought that
this would have the effect of misleading the authorities into
thinking we were going to squat in that borough. We intended
that this march should publicize and announce a *fait accompli*
that had occured a week or two earlier, the idea being that the
families would move in quite normally either one or two
weekends before 9 February. The sudden announcement on 9
February that the families had been living in the houses concerned for a week or more would, we considered, put the
council in a very awkward situation. In fact this plan did not
work, because neither we nor the families were ready to squat
at the beginning of February.

Secrecy was essential, as a leak would mean that we would
arrive at the houses to find them guarded by police or council
officials. Thus only about ten people were told where the squat
was to be. Most of the Supply and Transport Committee, who
spent weeks collecting furniture and food, did not know where
it was all going until the night before. The Workman's Committee had to know as they had to enter the houses and
measure up every door and window in order to prepare barricades of the right sizes. They spent weeks going round demolition sites and derelict houses collecting wood and metal, and
sawing these up into strips of exactly the correct length. The
Planning Committee co-ordinated all this and also looked
again into the legal position. As at the Hollies a most important part of our planning was to cover ourselves legally.
Firstly, as we intended to turn water and electricity on in the
houses we had to avoid being prosecuted under the Theft Act.
We decided that the way to do this was to take a meter reading
before turning on the power and write immediately to the

London Electricity Board giving them this reading and offering to pay for all the power consumed plus any fixed charge they demanded. As a constituent part of theft is dishonesty we felt that this was the way round this charge. It is worth recording here that this proved to be effective. At one stage in the Redbridge campaign the police, frustrated at being unable to pin any charge on us, tried to get nine of our number convicted of theft. When the case came up at North-east London Quarter Sessions the fact that we had taken meter readings on entering the house, plus the fact that we had given the Electricity Board a cheque for £100 and told them to take any amount they felt we owed them from it, was sufficient to secure an acquittal.

Eviction was our next worry and another legal point that had to be considered. There were various ways in which the council could use the courts to get us removed from the houses. We found ways of avoiding all these; just how we did this will become clear during my account of the campaign. But what of immediate forcible eviction? Our research into the law had convinced us that this was illegal, for although a person may use reasonable force to eject a trespasser, it is an offence under the Forcible Entry Act of 1381 forcibly to remove anyone *who claims and takes control and possession* of land without a court order, even though the possession may be wrongful. It is enough to quote one authority for this here: the Forcible Entry Act says that it is an offence forcibly to enter land in the possession of another, and Archbold's Criminal Pleading, page 1,307, states quite clearly that,

even if (one) has a right of entry still his asserting that right 'with strong hand or multitude of people' is equally an offence within the statute as if he had no right.

It was decided then that the best protection against an immediate eviction was to prepare a leaflet – a 'legal warning' – telling the authorities this. Despite this we still believed that the most dangerous period was the first half an hour when the immediate reaction of the police, thinking that they had the right to do so would be to rush in and remove us. That is why we decided that we needed the protection of barricades as well.

All our legal arrangements were handled by the Planning Committee, as was the job of arranging everything with the families involved and obtaining from them as much information as we could about their plight so as to be able to publicize it. A number of families at the Council Buildings Hostel in Poplar were interested in squatting, and we explained to them all that we were not politicians and thus could promise nothing except our support, come what may. We could also add that in our judgement the struggle was 'winable'. After considerable discussion, both among ourselves and with the families, it was finally decided that three families should squat.

Ben and Margaret Beresford had seven children. They had lived at Council Buildings for nearly four years and had recently received a letter to say that they were not even on the list to be 'considered' for a house. Apart from the overcrowding – seven children and two adults in three rooms – the damp and depressing nature of the place and the sanitary conditions made normal life impossible. At Council Buildings it is literally possible to sit on the toilet and cook a meal, so close is the cooker to the lavatory. It would be possible to sit on the toilet and wash, were there a bath and hot water. On top of all this Margaret had no gas and had been cooking for the family over a coal fire for two years. The Beresfords were keen to squat. We knew from the vicarage that Margaret was a determined woman and we also knew that Ben was ready for a struggle. Ben was fifty-eight and arthritic, finding a job for himself was therefore difficult. He knew all about squatting – he had helped the vigilante movement in Hastings in 1945.

The other two families were Paddy and Mary King with their one child, and Danny and Carol McNally and their child. Mary, like Margaret Beresford, had also been at the vicarage, so she also knew what squatting entailed. She and her family had lived at Council Buildings for nearly a year. The McNallys were somewhat different, they did not live in a hostel, but with Carol's mother. They had become homeless two and a half years earlier when Danny had injured his back while working on the Blackwall Tunnel. Since then four of

their children had been taken into care as there was no room at
Carol's mother's house for them. Squatting to the McNallys
could mean getting their children back.

Everything was ready: detailed plans had been laid; the
families had been briefed and knew what to expect. As our
plan to install the families a week or two prior to 9 February
did not materialize, our decision to mislead the authorities by
meeting at Manor Park Station became doubly important and,
fortunately, had the desired effect. We concurred with the false
impression created by giving interviews to the Newham local
papers and even by meeting the Housing Manager, Mr Pat
Davies, who asked us not to proceed with the demonstration
as Newham was doing all it could for the homeless. Of course
we refused, trying hard not to smile.

Not content with this we thought that we would take everybody completely by surprise by actually squatting on Saturday
8 February, a day before everyone expected us to. By Friday 7
February everything was ready. The houses had been checked
the night before and were still empty, with back windows open,
to enable easy and non-forcible entry. Numerous piles of wood
and metal, all labelled to fit particular windows of each house,
were laid out in my back garden. We had arranged to pick up
the families' furniture at 7 p.m. that evening in my van and in
a larger van hired by the Supply and Transport Committee.
That committee had also arranged for a pantechnicon to collect more furniture from all over London that day and to
arrive at my house later on that evening, where three dozen
people were to meet, in readiness for the next day's squat.

However, one thing occurred that no amount of careful planning could have foreseen. On the afternoon of 7 February the
sky opened and it snowed – and snowed – and snowed. As the
evening wore on the snow only got worse and so in the worst
blizzard I can remember two vans skidded and slipped their
way to Poplar to pick up all the families' furniture. Despite
everything a dozen people somehow got the three families'
belongings loaded into the vans which then chugged slowly
back to my house in Leytonstone.

There have been many times in the course of the campaign
when I have felt particularly emotional and the time we spent

loading the vans was one of them. It suddenly occurred to me that this could never be just another campaign – we were actually taking all the families' possessions into our vans; we were actually moving people's homes. What this meant hit me as it had never done before and, quite apart from any moral or political opinions, from that time on I knew that I could never even begin to understand how any human being could accept the job of evicting a family.

At about 10 p.m. the two vans arrived at my house, where the other people were waiting. Many of these were told for the first time that the squat was going to be in Redbridge rather than Newham. A little after we got back the pantechnicon arrived half full of furniture. Those of us present now had the job of arranging all the belongings and labelling them correctly to enable us to unload them quickly. At about midnight on 7 February about thirty people gathered in Hainault Road, a quiet road in Leytonstone, and loaded furniture from van to van. Fortunately by this time the snow had at last stopped, but the roads were covered in about two inches of it and were treacherously slippery. Residents must have wondered what on earth was going on. Eventually the job was completed; the furniture was arranged and labelled, together with large quantities of food, cans of fuel and sacks of coal, all to be used in case of a prolonged siege.

At about 2 a.m. on 8 February we settled down to try and get some rest, but with three dozen people crammed into one room, very few people slept. Less than three hours later we were all up again. The Workman's Committee drove off in a car to enter the houses while it was still dark. The reason for this was to enable the rest of us to be let in later through the front door, so that everything would look as normal as possible and also to give the 'workmen' time to re-connect the water and electricity supplies.

The rest of us started tying up the barricades and loading them into the van. The fact that they were covered in two inches of ice did not make this easy – but we managed it. At about 8 a.m. the families were collected and we were all ready to set off. A flat battery in the pantechnicon meant that it would not start, but even that did not put us out of our stride and thirty people pushing it, plus a push from the other van, soon got it going, even on the slippery road.

So far every hurdle had been surmounted and our convoy of vans and cars made for our targets, numbers 59, 67 and 34 Oakfield Road, Ilford. Just when it seemed that 'we had overcome' we were met by a further and completely unforeseeable obstacle. All the houses had been rechecked on the Thursday, but when we arrived at Oakfield Road on the Saturday morning we discovered that the council had ripped up the floor boards of number 34 and nailed them to the windows and door. This must have been done on the Friday – we were one day too late. We therefore now had only two houses, but flexibility had always been our strength. The Kings and McNallys doubled up in number 67, and the Beresfords took number 59. Quickly we unloaded all the furniture and started to put the barricades up.

When the police arrived half an hour later we were well entrenched in both houses – but not well enough. Our fear that the initial reaction of the police would be to remove us and stop to think afterwards proved well founded. Led by Inspector David Millam, they smashed their way into 59 Oakfield Road. I was in number 67 and the sight of the Beresfords walking out of the house with their seven children was heartbreaking. Then however came the assault on number 67 and this time our barricades held. We quickly blocked off the stairs and held the upper floor of the house, but it was a near thing. I shudder to think what might have happened if we had been removed from that house too.

The Beresfords took it all remarkably well. Later that day they were driven back to Council Buildings. They had suffered a setback, but later events were to show that it would take more than that to defeat them. In Ilford things quietened down after the initial panic. By the evening of 8 February we were able to come and go from 59 Oakfield Road quite freely and, early on Sunday morning 9 February, we reoccupied the house and put the McNallys into it, and again barricaded the stairs. The Kings then lived upstairs in number 67, while the McNallys lived upstairs in number 59. The only means of access was by rope ladder through the windows.

The next day, Sunday 9 February, about 200 people gathered at Manor Park Station ready to march 'to install homeless families in empty property'. After a short meeting we moved off and walked the two miles to Ilford. When we reached the Ilford central area, instead of leading the march straight to the street where the families were squatting, we led it on a conducted tour of the many empty houses in the area. As we marched we invited people to occupy a house. Eventually the march entered Oakfield Road, to be met by the Kings and McNallys waving from their windows. There were a number of speeches from the 'occupied' houses and while these were going on Dave Pearce, whom I had met at Suttons Hostel about a week earlier, got together a small group of squatters and hurried round to Cleveland Road, the next road along from Oakfield Road. In one of the empty houses there a window had been left open. Dave went in, while the rest of us barricaded the stairs with the wood lying plentifully nearby. When the rest of the marchers got to hear of this an enormous cheer went up and they followed us round to Cleveland Road. 'I'm occupying this house until Redbridge Council rehouse my family,' Dave declared. 'I'm fed up with their promises and I'm fed up with Suttons Hostel.' Leaflets quoting legal authorities and the Forcible Entry Acts were quickly given to the senior police officers present, but the police now knew what was going on and so did not panic as they had done the day before. There was no attempt to remove those who had occupied the house.

The meeting in Cleveland Road continued but I went back to Oakfield Road to see how things were there. Suddenly I heard another loud cheer, coming from Cleveland Road. Someone rushed round into Oakfield Road and announced to us that yet another house had been taken over. I quickly went back to Cleveland Road and saw that a group of West Ham anarchists had occupied an empty house owned by the Post Office. The police seemed worried about this. An inspector approached me: 'Mr Bailey, that house is being used as a store-room; it is entirely different from the rest, there are confidential files in it; if you don't get them out you'll be charged with warehouse breaking.' I pointed out to him that I neither would nor could do this. The people in the house had overheard the conversation, however, and yelled down: 'Rubbish – there are only a few old calendars in here.' At this the police withdrew their threat, and things quietened down.

I have been attending demonstrations for years, but for sheer spontaneous action and a feeling of comradeship this one, although small, would take a lot of beating. Gradually the supporters drifted away, leaving only about fifty people behind. Later that evening we held a meeting at 59 Oakfield Road and drew up a guard rota for both houses. Most of the organizers of the weekend's events were by this time falling asleep as they had not been to bed for two nights, but new arrivals carried the meeting along and many declared their intention of staying permanently in Ilford to guard the families.

The days following the demonstration are difficult to describe properly. The events are easy enough to record, but to capture the spirit that grew up is another matter. Our demonstration achieved widespread publicity both on television and in all the national newspapers. Indeed, all that week we remained in the press. Dozens of journalists made the climb up the rope ladders, still the only means of access to the houses, to interview the families. Thames Television's 'Today' team also paid a visit. Alf Williams expressed the determination of the whole campaign when he said, in reply to an interviewer's query, that if necessary he would still be guarding the house 'next Christmas'. He had no intention of leaving until he was no longer needed. Jim Radford, who regularly made the journey up to Redbridge from his home in Kent and Malcolm Conn, both of whom had been involved since before the Hollies, were still fully committed to the campaign. Two members of the Ilford branch of International Socialism, Alan Reid and Sally James, also played a vital role in ensuring that all the many day-to-day problems that arose were tackled. It is worth noting here that both Alan and Sally left International Socialism because of the failure of that group to continue to support the squatters.

One television programme, 'Man Alive', was already making a documentary on the squatters. Their team had extensively filmed the preparations for the squat and now they continued to cover virtually every move we made. This proved useful as there is nothing more calculated to embarrass local authorities than a television camera constantly focused on them.

On Monday 10 February we had to take stock. One of the houses, 59 Oakfield Road, was a private house. We knew this when we occupied it, but did so because of the length of time it had been empty and because of the intention of the owners to let it as offices. The sign outside proclaiming 'offices to let' symbolized all the priorities that we rejected. 67 Oakfield Road was rather different; we had checked with the council minutes and knew that it was one of the houses that Redbridge Council was acquiring in preparation for their proposed redevelopment scheme. Conveyancing, however, takes months to finalize and in this case it had not yet been completed – technically the house was still not owned by the council. This presented us with a policy problem: should we stay in, or should we vacate the house? We were out primarily to pressurize councils and not individuals who owned the odd house. On the other hand we knew that if we moved out the council would, as soon as they acquired the house, rip up the floorboards and board the place up. We decided that our job was to insist that the council bought this house with the Kings living in it and allow them to stay.

The newly occupied houses in Cleveland Road became the centre for all those who had come on the demonstration – and stayed on to help. Dozens of spontaneous meetings and discussions took place at all hours of the day and night, while at Oakfield Road people took turns in guarding the families there. Alf Williams seemed to be a permanent guard, to see him sleep was rare. People arrived with food, furniture, clothing and everything we needed. One man, Carl Rosen, who owned a television shop, bought television sets for the families. He came on the demonstration on 9 February and has remained active in housing campaigns to this day. Someone else gave us a cooker. The McNally's house at 59 Oakfield Road had telephone wires laid on and we even tried to connect these up to lay on a telephone.

At one of the numerous meetings in Cleveland Road, on Tuesday 11 February at 2 a.m., someone reported that they had been given a 'tip off' by a neighbour about another empty house in that road. His information was that it was owned by the council and had been empty for a year. A group of us went to inspect it, getting in through an open window at the back. It was a large house and we immediately decided to occupy it. We knew that the Beresfords were keen to squat again and this seemed the ideal home for them. Thus at 2.30 a.m. on 11 February we took possession of 43 Cleveland Road and the next day we went up to the Town Hall to offer to pay rent for the house. Needless to say, our offer was refused, despite the fact that the council intended to leave this particular house empty until 1977 – even supposing the redevelopment plan obtained ministry approval, and was on schedule.

Indeed it was at this point that the 'property owners panic' started. By the afternoon of 11 February Redbridge Council were handing out High Court injunctions restraining those named on them from remaining in wrongful occupation of 43 Cleveland Road. Unfortunately for the council we had already worked out a way to render these ineffective. Most of the people named on the injunctions had never been near the house and those who were in occupation, although named in both the *Evening Standard* and the *Evening News* on 11 February, were not named on the injunctions. Those people named and who were there simply left the house, and others took their place.

On Wednesday 12 February, Alf Williams, Dave Pearce and myself met the Redbridge Housing Manager, Mr David Perry. We told him what we wanted – rent books for the families and the opening up of the empty houses in Ilford. The meeting did not achieve much, except that Mr Perry gave Dave Pearce an assurance that he and his family would be rehoused 'by the end of the month'. One squatter family was thus made happy.

The outbreak of 'property owners panic' was now taking on quite ludicrous proportions. Alf Williams and I were receiving writs and injunctions galore. One ordered us not to trespass on North Weald Aerodrome, where there were apparently seventy-four empty army homes. Another told us to 'keep off' Theydon Grove Estate in Epping and not to 'conspire with others' to enter it. The fact that I had never heard of Theydon Grove seemed to be of little consequence to the agents for that estate.

An injunction to be taken more seriously, however, was one that arrived restraining Jim Radford, myself and the Kings from continuing to trespass on 67 Oakfield Road. To Jim and me this was of no consequence, but to the Kings it was vitally important that this should be evaded as it meant that if they continued to live in the house they would be liable to be committed to prison for contempt of court. Mere avoidance of service of the injunctions would not be a good enough way of evading them, as the writ servers could then apply to the court for substituted service – that is by announcing the injunctions in the local and national press. It was necessary therefore to fool the writ servers into thinking that the injunctions had been served, when in fact they had not. Luckily as soon as the server arrived he pounced on me and, although this meant I had been served, it also gave us prior warning, and a few minutes to put our plan into action. On seeing a woman come out of 67 Oakfield Road the server approached her. 'Mrs King?' he asked, and on receiving an affirmative reply he served the injunction on her. A similar process was adopted with 'Mr King'. Unfortunately for the server the man and the woman were not Mr and Mrs King. The injunctions were immediately torn up, the Kings never saw them and so were not in contempt of court.

Redbridge Borough Council was also in a state of panic. I have already described how they had started to board up empty houses on the day before our arrival in Ilford. Towards the end of February they apparently considered this was not enough to 'deter' the squatters. After all, boards could be removed and a few floorboards easily nailed back, so the anti-squatter brigade on the council decided that the interiors of their three dozen empty houses should be destroyed. During the last week in February and the first week in March, council workmen, employed by the Borough Engineers Department, entered the houses armed with pickaxes, saws, choppers and so on, and set to work. After spending anything up to a day in each house they moved on to the next, leaving their trail of destruction behind them. Floorboards were not only removed – they were smashed up. Ceilings were chopped out, stairs destroyed, even sinks and toilets were smashed in some houses, electricity and water fittings were ruined. In short each house became more or less a shell – four walls and wreckage. This was Redbridge Council's latest anti-squatter measure. The cost to the rate payers amounted to £2,520. The 'public spirited' men of the council planned to leave houses in this state from February 1969 until some time between 1971 and 1976.

Meanwhile we squatters tried to continue our work despite all the harassment. Luckily we had Alf Williams for whom nothing was too much trouble. So when the Ministry of Social Security withheld benefit from squatting families, it was Alf who sorted it out – arranging with the manager that families 'under the auspices' of the Squatters Campaign would be paid, providing Alf or I signed a statement declaring that they were squatters. And when the local schools would not accept the children of squatting families it was Alf who made them do so and carry out their duties under the 1944 Education Act. This was quite an amusing saga. The *Ilford Pictorial* on Wednesday 19 February carried a front page headline declaring 'Squatters' Children Barred from School'. The very next day, Thursday 20 February, the *Ilford Recorder* announced 'School – Squatters Win'. Alf had brought about this change of face simply by accompanying the parents and their children to school – and refusing to move until the headmistress accepted them. Emergency discussions between her and the Chief Education Officer, Mr Gilbert Miles, resulted in the education authorities backing down; the alternative would have been for the police to carry people out of a primary school and this, to the authorities, was apparently even worse than having squatters' children in their school.

In the face of all this we carried on a propaganda campaign. We produced leaflets, held marches, heckled council meetings and, most important of all, moved in more families. Ben and Margaret Beresford and their seven children were moved into 43 Cleveland Road on Sunday 16 February; Jim and Shelly Corridon, a young couple from Brixton who had approached us, were moved into 67 Oakfield Road, beneath Paddy and Mary King. Yvonne Parker, a young divorcee from Dagenham, moved herself and her three children into 59 Oakfield Road, beneath Carol and Danny McNally.

The real battle, however, came over 43 Cleveland Road, where the Beresfords were settling into their first real home for many years. I have already described how we avoided the injunctions that the council had taken out. Their next move was to adopt a really archaic procedure, in an attempt to remove us from the premises. No doubt frustrated by our 'legal notice' quoting the Forcible Entry Act and warning landlords not to attempt a forcible eviction without a court order, the council now tried to use these acts against us. On Monday 17 February they applied to the Barking Magistrates Court for restitution of 43 Cleveland Road, under the Forcible Entry Acts of 1391 and 1429.

This move must be explained. I have already described how we had been careful to avoid breaking the Forcible Entry Act of 1381, as a breach of it could only have resulted in our prosecution. Such a breach would also have given the owners the opportunity to apply to the local magistrates for restitution of the property. Briefly, this means that if a landowner can prove that somebody has forcibly taken possession of his land, although he himself cannot forcibly retake possession, he has a speedy remedy by applying to the local magistrates to clear the premises, to cast those in possession into the nearest jail and to hand the property back to him. This power dates from the Forcible Entry Act of 1391. As I have said, we did not enter 43 Cleveland Road forcibly and even the council had to admit this. At Barking Magistrates Court on 17 February, however, the council claimed that we were 'forcibly detaining' (i.e. holding) the premises, contrary to the Forcible Entry Act of 1429, and on this basis they asked the magistrates to clear the house and hand it back to them.

Fortunately I happened to be in Barking Court that morning and I heard the council's barrister making his application. I jumped up from the public gallery declaring that there was no forcible detainer at 43 Cleveland Road. The magistrates declined to make an order of restitution immediately, but decided to go and view the premises to see for themselves whether or not we were forcibly holding them. Now the legal position on this is very clear. It is *not* a forcible detainer within the meaning of the 1429 Act merely to shut the door and refuse to

allow the owner access to the property and this is all we had
done at 43 Cleveland Road. We had used no force to frighten
the owner away or deter him from coming near; we had
merely refused to allow the council to enter.

However, with the decision of the magistrates to view the
premises another legal evading tactic had to be used, for although it is not forcible detainer to refuse to allow the owner
into the premises, it *is* forcible detainer to refuse to allow the
magistrates in if they desire to enter to 'view'. Thus on the
afternoon of 17 February 1969 Ilford saw the drama of my
running down Cleveland Road to tell the occupants that the
magistrates were on their way, and must be let in. Three
minutes later the magistrates arrived, rapped on the door and
demanded entrance. The door was opened and in they went.
Ten minutes later they left. On Friday 21 February the magistrates announced their decision in open court – they were not
going to hand back the premises to the council. Another legal
attempt by the council to remove us had been thwarted.

The importance of this cannot be stressed too much. This
could have been the council's most effective legal weapon, as it
was (but is not necessarily now) the only legal way of obtaining
an order to clear *property*. All the other legal weapons in the
council's armoury had to be directed at named *people*, who
could be swapped around. (Under the new High Court order it
is now possible in *some* circumstances, but not all, to obtain a
possession order against unnamed defendants.[1])

. The Legal Department of the Redbridge Borough Council
must also have realized the effectiveness of this weapon, for
following the refusal of the Barking magistrates to act, the
council sought an Order of Mandamus from the High Court,
which would compel the magistrates to do so. This was heard
in the Queens Bench Divisional Court on 6 March 1969, before
the Lord Chief Justice, Lord Parker. The Beresfords, who were
still living happily at 43 Cleveland Road, were represented by
Mr Victor Levene. Mr Levene argued on a number of legal
grounds that it would be wrong for the Court to grant the
Order of Mandamus. His main point was, simply, that there
was no forcible detainer at 43 Cleveland Road. Mr Levene was

1. See page 128ff.

successful in preventing the court granting the order, but rather than rule outright in favour of the squatters, Lord Parker adjourned the case *sine die* and told the council to apply for a possession order in the normal way. A further legal attempt by the council had thus failed to remove us from the house.

While all this was happening we carried on a publicity campaign against the council which concentrated on two main points. First, we argued, there was no logical reason why the Beresfords should not be allowed to stay in the house and pay rent, as they had continually offered to do. There was no question of them jumping the queue as the council had no intention of using the house. This, in fact, proved a powerful argument that obtained us much sympathy. If we had squatted in houses that were going to be used, the squatting families could have been accused of jumping the queue and pushing another family out. By squatting only in houses that were to be left empty we avoided this criticism (although the council still tried to use it) and increased our moral justification for squatting. The second main point on which we based our propaganda was the council's house-wrecking policy. This house-wrecking aroused widespread criticism, in the borough, in the press and on television, particularly in view of the fact that the redevelopment plan for which these houses were being acquired had not been approved by the ministry and there were over 2,000 objections to be considered at the Ministry of Housing public inquiry, which was finally held in June 1970.

While our struggle with the Redbridge Borough Council was going on we also became involved in a minor struggle with the Greater London Council. As I have already said more families were now contacting us asking us to help them squat. One such family was the Mercers, who were living under threat of eviction in a flat in Stamford Hill. Their landlord had made life as unpleasant as possible for them by cutting off the water and electricity. They were keen to squat immediately, and phoned me up about five times a day until we arranged it.

We had been told of a house owned by the GLC in Courtland Avenue, Ilford, that had been empty for two years. Entering through an open window at the rear we ascertained that it was in first-class condition and we decided that it would be an excellent house for the Mercers to squat in. On 26 February, therefore, the Mercers arrived in Ilford with all their furniture loaded into a lorry and we took them to Courtland Avenue, where one of our groups had already entered through the usual window. The lorry drew up outside the house and we walked up the path with the Mercers' furniture; our comrade inside opened the door – and we were in! Everything went so smoothly that no one even realized that we were squatters and, within half an hour, the Mercers were settling into their new home.

Redbridge Council had clearly been shaken by our skill at avoiding their legal attempts to evict us from 43 Cleveland Road. Further, our success in publicizing their house-wrecking policies had embarrassed them considerably. The result was that on 17 March 1969 the council's Town Centre Redevelopment Committee met and decided on a policy change regarding houses acquired by them in preparation for the redevelopment plan. The idea was that any future houses acquired by the council would not be left empty, but would be offered to the welfare departments of other boroughs for use as temporary accommodation, the other boroughs being responsible for repairs and so on. This could have been of major importance had it materialized, because if other London boroughs had followed suit and used their empty short-term houses in this way, then all hostels and halfway houses in London could have been closed down. People in need of temporary accommodation could have been given shelter in the empty houses instead. This policy change by the council was thus an important victory for the squatters campaign and, on 21 March, Jim Radford and I met the deputy Town Clerk of Redbridge, Mr Findlay, to discuss the scheme.

This discussion was of considerably more use than any previous attempts by us to talk with the council, but one bone of contention remained. The council insisted that this plan would apply only to houses to be acquired in the future. Empty houses already owned by the council would not be included in it. This meant that the council was determined to continue with its efforts to repossess 43 Cleveland Road which, as it was already owned by the council, would therefore not be included in the scheme. The council could present no logical reason for this, particularly as 43 Cleveland Road would not be needed for the redevelopment plan until 1976 at the earliest. Nevertheless Mr Findlay told Jim Radford and me that the council still wanted the Beresfords out of the house and that they would be proceeding with an application for possession, due to be heard at Ilford County Court on 2 April.

While Jim Radford and I were talking to the deputy Town Clerk, a strange telephone call came through to his office for me. I spoke to my former wife who told me that there was an eviction taking place at Courtland Avenue. Jim and I were puzzled by this and, quickly drawing our discussion to a close, we hurried round to the Mercers' house. On arrival we saw about eighteen people, including squatters, policemen and GLC officials. Ricky Mercer and Alan Reid, one of the squatters group, rushed up to me and told me that there had been an eviction attempt. I could see the Mercers were in an extremely agitated state; I looked round and saw pieces of furniture over the front lawn, and the front door of the house smashed. 'Six of these bailiffs there were,' said Ricky, 'they smashed open the door with long crowbars and rushed into the house. They beat us up, hit us with the bars and started throwing the furniture out. Two of them rushed upstairs and dragged Karen out of bed and threw her on the floor.' When Olive, his wife, spoke to me she confirmed that six men had in fact smashed their way into the house, and hit her in the stomach with iron bars, and I further discovered that the eviction had only been terminated when a doctor had arrived and confirmed the Mercers' claims that five-year-old Karen Mercer was ill in bed with scarlet fever, and was not to be moved. This had meant that these 'bailiffs', who had no court order whatsoever, had had to call off the eviction attempt and content themselves with standing across the road and hurling abuse at all present. At one point they had taken photographs of the squatters and warned that if they were caught on the street 'they would be smashed to the ground'.

At another point, when Olive Mercer had gone round to the

Beresfords at 43 Cleveland Road to ask for help, they had followed her and waved their fists up at that house and shouted 'You're next, you bastards.' In addition to Karen Mercer being ill with scarlet fever, Olive Mercer was four months pregnant; as a result of the blows with the iron bars she started to haemorrhage. After the furniture had been put back in the house and the bailiffs had driven off in their cars, Olive Mercer went to see her doctor about this. Unfortunately his surgery was closed, and the only 'treatment' Olive received that evening was to be accosted by the 'bailiffs' on her way home, assaulted, pushed against a wall and further terrorized. In the light of all this it is small wonder that one of the squatters, Alan Reid, who is no small-fry, said to me, 'I've seen bailiffs; these weren't bailiffs, they were the real heavy mob; they deal in terror, and they sure frightened me.'

And so Karen Mercer's scarlet fever saved the Mercers from eviction. Efforts by myself and others to discover just who the 'bailiffs' were proved unsuccessful at that stage, but I did manage to discover that the GLC official in charge was Mr H. W. Moss, the Area Valuer, whose office is in Ilford High Road, and that he was acting on instructions from Mr Roland Freeman, chairman of the GLC Finance Committee[1] and Mr Kenneth Blessley, the chief Valuer and Estate Agent for the GLC. That night I spoke on the telephone to Mr Horace Cutler, GLC Housing Committee chairman. Both Ricky Mercer and I told him what had happened. He assured us that he was 'shocked' and would certainly 'look into the matter'. Mr Cutler's 'looking into the matter' amounted to the Mercers receiving a letter from Mr Neil Thorne, their GLC representative, asking them to meet him at his office. Mr Thorne's interest in the affair was equally fleeting – consisting of one meeting with the Mercers and a question to Mr Roland Freeman at the GLC meeting on 26 March.

Mr Freeman's written reply contains an amazing statement. He said that the eviction had been undertaken without a court order as

1. I should explain that this house came under the auspices of the Finance Committee as it had been repossessed by the GLC after mortgage default.

civil proceedings through the County Court would normally take several months and I was advised that the Council could not wait such a long period ... it was accordingly decided to remove the Squatters ...[1]

In other words: 'The legal way doesn't suit us, as it takes too long, so we'll ignore the law and do the job quickly.' I sincerely hope that Mr Freeman will remember his words of 26 March 1969 the next time a political demonstrator is in court for feeling that an issue is urgent enough to warrant direct action. I also spoke to the deputy Town Clerk of Redbridge, Mr Findlay, on the evening of the eviction attempt. He also assured me that he was 'shocked' at what I had told him, and added that the Redbridge Council would never do anything like it. Mr Findlay's 'never' lasted just over one month.

In the opinion of the squatters campaign and of our legal advisors, this behaviour was illegal. The law is quite clear: one must not enter and repossess land without a court order 'with strong hand or multitude of people', even if one has a legal right of entry. The reason for this law is that private individuals should not be allowed to employ armies to fight over land, but that disputes should be settled through the courts which will re-possess the land for the rightful party. With this in mind, there-fore, the squatters adopted a policy of legal retaliation against the GLC. On three occasions Alan Reid, the Mercers and I applied for summonses at both Barking and Stratford Magi-strates Courts against the organizers of the evictions – Mr Moss, Mr Freeman and Mr Blessley – alleging 'forcible entry' and 'riotous assembly'. These applications were refused and the eviction attempt thus went without condemnation from the courts, the police or the officers and councillors of the GLC.

Notwithstanding the fright suffered by the Mercers, the campaign in Redbridge was riding on the crest of a wave. We had so far avoided all the council's attempts to remove us from their property and had forced them to make an 'offer' regard-ing their empty houses. Early in March we had moved Mrs Jenny Garcia and her child into yet another house – 23 Audrey Road. Initially we believed this house to be owned by

1. Reply to Question no. 1,223 in the council minutes, 26 March 1969.

Redbridge Council, but we later discovered that the conveyancing had not been completed and so technically the council had not quite acquired the house. We knew, however, that as soon as they did so they would wreck its interior, so we decided, after some discussion, that our job was to remain in occupation and to campaign to stop the council from wrecking 23 Audrey Road by forcing them to complete the deal for the house and then to utilize it for housing purposes.

Another point which greatly inspired the campaign was that squatting had produced results for some families. Mrs Parker, at 59 Oakfield Road, was given a house in a new town, while the Corridons were given a council flat in Brixton. Clearly the authorities were being pushed into doing the job they ought to have been doing already – rehousing families. The Kings and the McNallys were still squatting, but the McNallys had also achieved a considerable success – they had been told by the owner that they could stay at 59 Oakfield Road for six months. This had enabled them to get their four children out of care and so, for the first time in two and a half years, the McNally family were united.

However, the council was still doing its utmost to remove us. The main bone of contention between us and the Redbridge Council remained the Beresfords in 43 Cleveland Road. The council were determined to remove them and filed an application for possession, due to be heard at Ilford County Court on 2 April. An attempt at the council meeting on 1 April by Councillor Tony Young to get the council to suspend their application went unsupported as a result of Alderman Harold Cowan, the chairman of the Town Centre Redevelopment Committee, revealing considerable 'confidential' information obtained about the Beresfords passed to him by Camden social workers. So much for professional confidentiality! On 2 April the council were successful and Judge Stockdale granted them their order and told the Beresfords to hand over possession of 43 Cleveland Road within fourteen days. It is also worth mentioning here that the judge also sternly told the council's solicitor that he was of the opinion that the Beresfords should be permanently rehoused.

Meanwhile Jim Radford had contacted the Welfare Department of the Camden Council, the authority responsible for the Beresfords. Jim suggested that they could solve the deadlock by accepting the Redbridge 'offer' of the empty houses and then nominate the Beresfords for one of these. Under these circumstances Jim said that he felt that the Beresfords might be willing to vacate 43 Cleveland Road, but that we all knew that they would definitely not do so if it meant returning to Council Buildings. He went on to say that the squatters' supporters would not accept any suggestion that meant that Ben and Margaret and their children would have to return to the hostel they hated. The Camden 'Welfare' Department were not interested in Jim's suggestion. Indeed they were not even interested in utilizing any of the empty houses offered by Redbridge at all.

Such was the way of welfare.

There were a number of heated discussions among the squatters following Judge Stockdale's decision. We had until 16 April to decide what to recommend to the Beresfords. There were those who wanted to stay and fight the court bailiffs and police who would come to enforce the court order. On the other hand there were those who felt that while we were but a small number of people and not a mass movement such a policy would be disastrous, and that we should, therefore, defeat the council by trickery, rather than by a confrontation *on the council's own terms* at this stage. I strongly supported the latter course, as did most of the people who had been involved for any length of time. This was not because we were afraid of a confrontation, but because we were out to win this campaign and such a confrontation could not be won. It was decided, I am glad to be able to write, that we should adopt trickery, not out of cowardice or because of any principled opposition to heroic defences where they were necessary, but because we realized that while we were weak and small in number it was our one way of beating Redbridge Council.

The County Court possession order was thus to be evaded rather than fought. On Sunday 13 April we brought the Fleming family into Ilford, in readiness for what was to follow. Chris and Mary Fleming had contacted us a few days previ-

ously. They were desperate to squat as they had nowhere to
live; they had been staying with friends, but now had to leave.
They were on no council's lists as they had moved around too
much, and in order to get on a council list a family must be
resident in an area for a considerable time. For the Flemings,
then, squatting was the only answer and on Sunday 13 April
they moved temporarily into 23 Audrey Road, Ilford, with
Mrs Garcia.

On Tuesday 15 April the Beresfords did what Judge Stockdale ordered them to do: they vacated 43 Cleveland Road and
handed over possession to the council at 4 p.m. At 4.05 p.m.,
before the council had repossessed the house, the Fleming
family moved in and took possession. The Beresfords, meanwhile, took possession of another empty council house, 18
Grosvenor Road, Ilford. In broad daylight one of our group
found a way into the premises and the Beresfords and their
furniture followed. When the police arrived, 18 Grosvenor
Road was no longer an empty house, so they went away again
after asking us not to park our vans loaded up with furniture
on the wrong side of the road. We had thus pulled off a terrific
coup, and evaded the council's final legal weapon. As the
Ilford Recorder announced on Thursday 17 April 'Squatters
play musical chairs with the Council.' On the morning of
Wednesday 16 April I visited the Town Hall with the Flemings
to tell the council what we had done and there I spoke to Mr
Patrick Walsh, senior legal assistant in the Town Clerk's department. He was stunned. 'This means we've got to start
again,' he said. In fact the situation for Redbridge Council was
even worse than they realized. As no council would accept
responsibility for the Flemings, if Redbridge Council evicted
them they would, at the very least, have to provide them with
temporary accommodation, as laid down by the National
Assistance Act.

Our family swapping undoubtedly staggered the council,
who had always feared that it might happen, but never really
imagined us having the cheek actually to do it. 'They've gone
too far this time,' said Mr Candy, the deputy Housing Manager, in the *Ilford Express*, 18 April 1969. And yet it must be
remembered that not only had we broken no laws, we were

also not contravening any court order, writ or injunction. We had completely and absolutely twisted up and defeated the council legally.

We were cock-a-hoop and very confident now, so we decided to move in more families. Mr and Mrs John Byrne and their two children were installed in an empty house in Brittannia Road, Ilford. The Byrnes had lived for the preceeding nine months in Council Buildings, Poplar, and this hostel was fast getting on top of Ann Byrne. The house we moved them into, number 48, was in a similar state to 23 Audrey Road – the council were to acquire it for their redevelopment plan, but the legal formalities had not yet been completed. Another family had also contacted us – Mr and Mrs Wilson and their three children from Stepney. They did not live in a hostel, but had one small room in Royal Mint Square, in which they ate, slept, cooked, washed and did just about everything except go to the toilet (this they shared with ten other families). Despite these appalling conditions they had no chance of being re-housed for at least five years, so we moved the Wilsons into 50 Ley Street, Ilford, an empty house owned by Harrison Gibsons Ltd, the large furniture store.

Another family that had contacted us was Mrs Patricia McNeil, who had one three-year-old daughter. Pat, a young woman separated from her husband, had literally nowhere to go after 18 April, as on that day she had to leave the flat she had been staying in. On 17 April we moved her temporarily into 23 Audrey Road, and on 20 April we embarked on what was to be our *coup de grâce*. On that day, in broad daylight, we occupied 26 Britannia Road, one of the council-owned houses that had been wrecked inside by council workmen. We spent all that day unboarding the windows, re-laying the floorboards, building a new staircase, reconnecting the wires and pipes and generally making the place habitable again. By the evening we had completed the ground floor, and even made a start on the first floor. It was almost a miracle. We had actually rebuilt the interior of the house.

On the evening of 20 April we moved in some of Mrs McNeil's furniture, and made plans to replaster the ceiling on the following day. The actual repairing of a house that the council had wrecked was something that we would not have dreamed of even a month earlier: but now we had completed the bulk of it in only one day. It was a master-stroke and, following our 'swap' at 43 Cleveland Road, one which would really astound the council. Mrs McNeil was an excellent person to move into 26 Britannia Road as, like the Flemings, she was on no council list and so if Redbridge Council evicted her they would have to provide her with temporary accommodation too. This idea of 'lumbering' the council with responsibility was another weapon in our armoury. It was all very well for the council to try to remove the Beresfords from council property and then send them back to Council Buildings, but to evict families and by doing so give themselves additional responsibilities was another matter. At the beginning of April the Mercers had voluntarily vacated 81 Courtland Avenue, as the GLC had granted a mortgage on the house to a man who had been trying to obtain one for a long time. As he, too, was living in poor conditions the Mercers had decided to leave in order to let him move in. The Mercers then moved into a halfway house run by Redbridge Council. This had really embarrassed the council and their efforts to make Hackney Borough Council rehouse the Mercers had to be seen to be believed.

There is no doubt that the Redbridge Council had really been rocked by our activities of the week. I heard later that there had been a real fuss in the Town Hall over our repairing 26 Britannia Road. Someone had their knuckles rapped for not wrecking the house sufficiently.

That we were equally rocked (and shocked) by the council's reply is also true.

5. Redbridge: Part II

On 17 April 1969 the Town Centre Redevelopment Committee
of Redbridge Borough Council met. This meeting must enjoy
the dubious distinction of being just about the most destructive
meeting of any committee of Redbridge Council for a considerable time. Two decisions taken by those present prompt
me to make that statement. The first concerned the council's
'offer' of empty houses in the Ilford central area to the welfare
departments of other boroughs. It may be remembered that this
'offer' had been made on 17 March – exactly one month
earlier. At the meeting on 17 April it was withdrawn on the
alleged grounds that, 'The majority of the London Boroughs
do not wish to participate'[1] in the scheme. This excuse for
withdrawing the offer is, to say the least, extremely thin. The
same council minute clearly states that the London Borough
of Newham had expressed a desire to co-operate, while sixteen
authorities were yet to reply (after all one month in local
authority committee meeting terms is but a short time). Fourteen authorities had declared that they were not interested in
the scheme and somehow this fourteen became a 'majority'.
Now I do not wish to exonerate these fourteen authorities that
were not interested, but their refusal to participate in the
scheme should not be held by Redbridge Council to be a sufficient reason to drop it. Sixteen boroughs were still to reply and
yet the idea was dropped. I think it is quite clear that the
Redbridge Council were very quick to jump on any excuse that
they could to withdraw the 'offer' and not to use the houses.
The attitude of fourteen boroughs gave them the excuse – and
they took it.

The second important decision of the Town Centre Redevelopment Committee meeting on 17 April was concerned

1. Council minute 2,630 – presented to the council 13 May 1969

with the squatters' continued occupation of 43 Cleveland Road. Faced with this defeat by our legal manoeuvrings the meeting of the 17 April decided to ignore the law and the courts and to employ 'professional bailiffs' to evict squatting families – the Flemings from 43 Cleveland Road and the Beresfords from 18 Grosvenor Road. The Town Clerk was instructed to hire the same firm that the GLC had used at 81 Courtland Avenue and Monday 21 April was set as 'eviction day'. It was further decided that following the eviction 43 Cleveland Road would be demolished and that this large double-fronted house, in a good state of repair and not needed until 1977 for the (proposed) redevelopment plan, was to be pulled down and never used again. At the same time there are four and a half thousand families on Redbridge Council's housing lists and over 2,000 of these are classified as being in urgent need. There is certainly, then, no moral justification for the council's policy, and there is even more certainly no legal ground for their proposed action. The Council's attitude amounted to: 'When the law does not suit us we can ignore it.'

At 6 a.m. on Monday 21 April welfare and children's officers, council workmen and police met in the council car park in Oakfield Road, Ilford. Also present were the 'professional bailiffs' especially hired to do the job. Mr Patrick Walsh, of the Redbridge Town Clerk's department was also there, as was Mr George Henry Green, the council's own bailiff. Only a few of those gathered knew exactly what was going to happen – Mr Walsh and Mr Green among them – but most of them must have had a pretty shrewd idea.

The Beresfords at 18 Grosvenor Road, were the first victims. A downstairs window was smashed, and the bailiffs rushed in, followed by police and welfare officers. Ben and Margaret were woken by the noise and before they knew what was happening their bedroom was full of men ordering them out, dragging out their furniture and throwing some out of the door and the rest out of the windows. The Beresfords had to dress with all this going on: a policewoman meanwhile was dealing with their seven children in the other room. All the Beresfords were taken to a waiting van and locked in. Such were the services provided by the welfare and children's officers. The Beresford's furniture was loaded into a lorry and they were all driven back to Council Buildings, Poplar and put back in the hands of the Camden Welfare Department: the department that had turned down the Redbridge 'offer' of empty houses; the department that had supplied all the confidential social workers' reports on the Beresfords to Alderman Cowan which he revealed in public. Mr Patrick Walsh supervised the eviction for Redbridge Council. There was no court order, nor any pretence of one: indeed, the Beresfords had never even been asked to leave the premises. The first 'request' was made when bailiffs broke into the house and charged into the Beresford's bedroom.

Next on the list were the Flemings at 43 Cleveland Road. Here George Henry Green was the council's officer-in-charge. The hired bailiffs gained entry this time by smashing open the front door, and rushing in carrying long iron bars. Two members of the London Squatters Campaign were asleep downstairs in the house. One of these, David Jenkins, was grabbed by the bailiffs while dressing and was beaten up. While one bailiff who stands about 6'-10" in height grabbed him from behind, another punched him about the body and face. Mr Jenkins spent the next two weeks in hospital with a broken jaw and for four weeks after that had his mouth wired up while it healed. The other squatter who saw this was so alarmed that she ran terrified from the house. While this had been happening more bailiffs had run upstairs and smashed open the door to the bedroom where the Flemings and their children slept. With about eight men in the room the Flemings were forced to get up and dress. The bedclothes were pulled off their children, who were then grabbed, shaken and dumped back on the bed. The Flemings agreed to 'leave quietly' if the bailiffs left their children alone. At one point Chris Fleming asked about a court order. The only reply he got from one of the bailiffs was, 'Are these your children? Keep your mouth shut if you know what's good for you and your family.' Chris did not repeat the request. As soon as the Flemings were out of bed the bailiffs smashed the beds up. More furniture was being thrown straight out of the window.

By this time some of the squatters group had begun to arrive outside 43 Cleveland Road; myself, Tony Mahony and Mrs McNeil were among them. We were told by the police that we would be arrested for causing a breach of the peace if we interfered. Eventually amid pushing, punching, swearing and furniture being thrown from the windows, the Flemings emerged from the house, looking shocked and terrified. Chris had had to carry the children down the stairs, as the bailiffs had already started to smash up the banisters. When Chris approached one bailiff and asked him how he could do such a job, he was told by the police 'not to get involved'. As the Flemings left the house the council workmen went in armed with pickaxes. All that day and for quite a few days after the sound of them smashing up the house could be heard.

The welfare and children's officers present at the eviction had of course to justify their existence. When the Flemings emerged from the house, the officers descended on them to offer the 'services' of their respective departments. The Flemings, obviously shattered by the dawn eviction, were invited to go to the Welfare Department offices in Clements Road, Ilford, for a cup of tea. In the end however the combined efforts of the Redbridge Welfare and Children's Departments could not even provide this. The door to the welfare offices was locked and after a few minutes' discussion as to the whereabouts of the key all the officers went away leaving the Flemings standing in the rain on the step of the offices with three members of the Squatters Campaign who then took the family to 23 Audrey Road where they were given as much comfort as possible.

Some of us then thought we had better see what had happened at 26 Britannia Road, the house we had prepared the day before and half-installed Mrs McNeil in. The house backed on to 23 Audrey Road so we entered through the back garden. We were too late however. While we had been with the Flemings at the welfare offices the bailiffs had swooped on the house, which had been left empty. We found all the furniture on the front lawn, and the bailiffs all around. Those of us who had entered the house were threatened and in the face of this we left the house. The council workmen with their pickaxes entered and, in order to stop us repairing it again, they spent as long that day destroying it as we had spent repairing it the previous day. Mr Walsh had supervised yet another successful eviction and one which, from the point of view of democratic procedure, is of particular interest. I have explained how the Town Centre Redevelopment Committee meeting of 17 April decided to employ 'professional bailiffs' to evict squatters from the other two premises. Clearly, as 26 Britannia Road had not at that time been occupied by squatters, it was not even mentioned at that meeting. On the morning of 21 April, however, the bailiffs were available and obviously quite ready for another eviction, so Mr Walsh escorted them to 26 Britannia Road. Someone on Redbridge Council must have instructed Mr Walsh to take the bailiffs there as well. Whoever that someone was, the decision to evict us from that house does not seem to have been taken with the authorization of any committee of Redbridge Council.

The evictions of 21 April were a serious blow to the squatters campaign in Redbridge. As unpleasant as they were, however, they were clearly not enough for the council which, during the rest of 21 April, continued its campaign against the families it had evicted. I have explained already that the council had been able to transport the Beresfords back to the care of the Camden Welfare Department, but the Flemings and McNeils came under no council's care. These two families were thus literally on the streets in Redbridge and, as I have said, the council had a legal *duty* under the 1948 National Assistance Act to provide them with emergency shelter. Later on that morning both the families went to the welfare offices (now open) to seek emergency accommodation. The attitude of the welfare officials earlier had left them fearful and worried and they both asked one member of the squatters campaign to remain with them during their interviews with the welfare workers. I think in the circumstances this was not an unreasonable request – these same welfare workers had watched the evictions, apparently unmoved by them, and then left the families standing on the doorstep of the welfare department after offering them a mere cup of tea. The welfare officials, however, would not hear of the idea, although I personally

assured them that my presence at the interview would be silent
and that I had no intention of interfering. The Welfare Officer,
Mr Cole, remained adamant: the families got no further than
the corridor of the Welfare Department officers. We therefore
left the building, informing Mr Cole that we would be back at 3
p.m. again to request temporary accommodation for the
families.

When we returned at 3 p.m. we were again met in the corridor, but this time Mr Ronald Hall, the chief Welfare Officer,
was present. The families again asked that they might have a
friend present at their interview and this request was again
refused. Worse, however, was to follow: Mr Hall then told the
families that the Town Clerk had instructed him not to offer
the families accommodation. When Jim Radford and myself
argued that the Welfare Department had a legal duty to provide accommodation, Mr Hall's only answer was that the
Children's Department would help the children. The implica-
tions of this remark were quite plain – no emergency shelter;
children in care. Not content with illegally and brutally evicting these families, the council now planned to snatch their
children from them. Fortunately more squatters were arriving
on the scene and we threatened to sit in the Town Hall and
welfare offices until the council carried out its duty. After
nearly three hours the council gave in. Mr Walsh from the Town
Clerk's department persuaded Mr Hall to interview the families with me present and offer them accommodation. The
families were thus taken to the council hostel in Grosvenor
Road, Ilford. By this time, however, both families were near to
breaking point and the rules of the hostel plus the discovery by
Mrs McNeil's daughter of a truncheon in a drawer in the
hostel were too much for them. Under no circumstances
would they allow themselves to be 'cared for' by the Redbridge
Welfare Department. We therefore had to make our own
emergency arrangements. Mrs McNeil joined Mrs Garcia at
23 Audrey Road, and the Flemings came to stay at my home.
Somehow we got through 21 April 1969.

On the evening of 21 April there were two meetings of a
vastly different character. One was a meeting of the Redbridge
Council Welfare Committee where, naturally, the subject of

the evictions was discussed. It is worth quoting from the minutes of this meeting[1] to illustrate just how interested in welfare were the members of the Redbridge Welfare Committee. On the subject of the Beresfords the committee reported that 'assistance had been afforded to one family to return to accommodation provided for them by the Camden Council and to the care of the Welfare Committee of that authority'. That was how the Redbridge Welfare Committee described the locking of the whole family in a van and the drive back to Poplar. The description of the 'services' offered to the Flemings and McNeils is even better: 'Temporary accommodation in Grosvenor Road, Ilford, had been offered to the other families and refused.' That was the report on the events of that day – from the abandoning of the Flemings on the Welfare Department steps, to the subtle threats of children in care, and the outlining of the hostel rules several hours later to the shattered families. The Welfare Committee then declared, 'We are of the opinion that all reasonable and necessary welfare assistance was made available to the families concerned,' and finally they resolved that 'the action taken by the appropriate officers be supported'.

Is any comment necessary?

The second meeting that took place that evening was a squatters meeting at 23 Audrey Road, Ilford. As news of the evictions spread many people came to Ilford to offer their support and we met to discuss what to do. Some of the wilder suggestions, like smashing up the Town Clerk's home received little support, but instead we decided to embark on a 'harassment' policy towards councillors and officials responsible for the evictions. The Town Clerk, Kenneth Nicholls, Mr Patrick Walsh, Alderman Harold Cowan and Mayor Sidney Gleed were the main people to be harassed. Late that night we visited the houses of all four of them and in three cases knocked on their doors and told them in no uncertain terms what we thought of the violence of the evictions. At Alderman Cowan's house we were unable to do this as he already had a police guard outside his house. All of them except Mr Walsh, whose

1. Minute 2,647 – presented to, and accepted by, the Council on 13 May 1969.

telephone number is ex-directory, started to receive telephone calls at all hours of the day and night (at least that is preferable to bailiffs) and various objects started to arrive at their houses – including wreaths, water tanks, rubbish, tailors dummies and much more. They also received a number of unexpected callers – plumbers, estate agents and undertakers to name but a few. It may be thought that these are unpleasant tactics: I would agree, but suggest that these are one hundred times more pleasant than the evictions these men had authorized.

On Tuesday 22 April at 7 p.m. eleven squatters again visited the home of the Town Clerk. On this occasion things did not go quite according to plan: we were all arrested, kept in Ilford police station overnight and taken before the Barking Magistrates Court the next morning, 'as people whose conduct disturbed the peace' to 'show cause why we should not be bound over to keep the peace', in accordance with powers given to police under the Justice of the Peace Act, 1361. The court refused a police request to bind us over immediately and adjourned the case to enable us to prepare our defence. This is not the place to enter into a long legal argument about binding over, but it is perhaps worthy of mention here that when this case was finally heard at Barking Court on 10 July I argued with some success that there was an irregularity in the procedure which meant that we should not be bound over to keep the peace. The magistrates immediately bound us over to be of good behaviour and also found us guilty of using insulting words, a charge that had subsequently been added. An appeal by three of us to the North-East London Quarter Sessions was partially successful, and resulted in a further appeal to the High Court. The technicalities of this are complex but not relevant here.

To return to the campaign against the council, I think it would be fair to say that these arrests at the Town Clerk's house had the effect of lessening our harassment, but certainly not of stopping it altogether. Those of us arrested certainly had to be more discreet, as one of our conditions of bail was that we did not harass members or officials of the Redbridge Borough Council.

Harassment, however, was not the only weapon we used to

hit back at the council. We also did everything in our power to publicize the violence of the evictions. A short eight-page pamphlet was produced at the beginning of May, which described both the evictions and the attitude of the Redbridge Welfare Department, and outlined the law on the subject. Copies were sent to all the councillors and aldermen, to see if any of them would now disassociate themselves from what their council had done. The pamphlet was also forwarded to the local and national press and to selected television programmes. The local press, of course, reported it, but more important, one national paper and one television programme investigated the whole affair. The television was 'Thames Today'. They showed long interviews with the Flemings, Mrs McNeil, David Jenkins (whose jaw was wired up), and myself. The journalist who investigated the affair was Alex Mitchell of *The Sunday Times*. He did something that we had been unable to do – he discovered the name of the firm of bailiffs. On Sunday 11 May his story was published naming Barrie Quartermain and his firm, Southern Provincial Investigations, as the 'anti-squatter commandos'. This information was of considerable importance, as it enabled us now to attempt to institute legal proceedings against the bailiffs.

We tried to do just this at Barking Magistrates Court on 20 May 1969. Mr Victor Levene applied for summonses on behalf of the evicted families, against Barrie Quartermain, Brian Morley (one of his men), Patrick Walsh, and George Henry Green (the council officer-in-charge of the evictions) for 'forcible entry' and 'riotous assembly'. The magistrate, Mr J. Train, refused the application on the grounds that the Forcible Entry Act of 1381 did not apply any longer. When Mr Levene pointed out that two cases involving this act had been heard in the high court earlier in the year, Mr Train remained unmoved. He gave no reason for refusing the 'riotous assembly' summonses. So Barking Magistrates Court was therefore prepared to allow another illegal eviction to go unchecked. We were not prepared to allow this to go on any longer so we decided to apply to the Queen's Bench Divisional Court (High Court) for an Order of Mandamus, to compel Mr Train to grant these summonses. We were granted leave by that court to do this and the application was heard on 2 December 1969; Mr Train was ordered to re-hear the applications. As Lord Parker, the Lord Chief Justice, said: 'The only proper course was for an Order of Mandamus to be directed to the justices requiring them to hear and determine the applications according to the law,' (Times Law Reports 2 December 1969, printed in *The Times* 3 December 1969). Mr Train had been told in no uncertain terms that the Forcible Entry Act was still in force. In addition to this, the Ilford police decided at last to act on the issue of David Jenkins's broken jaw. A warrant for the arrest of two bailiffs on charges of assault occasioning grievous bodily harm has been issued but as yet remains unserved, as it is on description only, the names of the bailiffs not being known. This, in fact, is a poor reason. The police have means of finding out names if they want them and furthermore I have now obtained a photograph of one of the men, who, because of his size, should not be difficult for the police to find.

If our pamphlet had any impact on the press and television, however, it certainly had little or none on members of the Redbridge Council. Councillor Tony Young had supported us all along, but at the council meeting on 13 May, despite the fact that every councillor and alderman had received the pamphlet, and despite the fact that it contained an invitation to them all to inspect sworn statements we had concerning the evictions and the actions of the Welfare Department, the only effect was that Councillor Fred Watts asked a question about the welfare of the families. A brief reply from Welfare Committee chairman, Mrs Marie Page, was enough to persuade him that the council had acted humanely and he, like the rest of the councillors, voted to accept the welfare report already referred to. Indeed, far from being influenced by the pamphlet, many of the councillors were quick to jump to the defence of the council.

Concerning the 'services' of the Welfare Department, Mrs Marie Page, chairman of that committee, could only say, 'We received a report from our Chief Welfare Officer which we were very glad to receive. I have nothing more to say' (*Ilford Pictorial*, page 5, 21 May 1969). And concerning the evictions,

the violence, David Jenkins's broken jaw, the punching, pushing and swearing, Councillor Edgar Harris could only retort,
'The bailiffs did their job and did it well' (*Ilford Pictorial*, page
5, 21 May 1969). That, at least, was the truth.

*

For a while our occupation of property was halted, and just
how much our morale was adversely affected by the evictions
can be seen from the fact that when we occupied three empty
council houses in Sandyhill Road, Ilford, on Sunday 27 April,
the council was able to repossess two on the Monday morning.
When Mr Green their bailiff arrived, we had left two of them
empty. The only incident occurred when two squatters sat in
Mr Green's car; Diarmuid Breanach and I were arrested for
insulting behaviour. We were found guilty on 22 December
1969 despite gross contradictions in the prosecution's evidence,
with the result that an appeal by me was successful. Also arising out of this incident I successfully applied for a summons
against Mr Green for assault. This has since been adjourned
sine die following an agreement to drop 'cross summonses'
between myself and Mr Green. The third house we vacated
voluntarily on 29 April when we were shown council minutes
that proved that the council intended to use the house itself
and had acquired a government grant to improve it.

On the other hand, although we were down, we were by no
means out. We still attended to the responsibilities that we
already had. The Flemings could not live in two rooms at my
house for long and we therefore made alternative arrangements for them. 67 Oakfield Road was at that time empty,
except for a few of our guards who were staying there; the
Corridons had been rehoused in Brixton as I have already said,
and the Kings had voluntarily returned to Council Buildings.
The latter family had a number of other problems in addition
to homelessness and they felt that a more stable and less tense
atmosphere would be better for them. On Sunday 24 April, in
addition to our abortive attempts to occupy houses in Sandyhill Road, we also moved the Flemings into 67 Oakfield Road,
where they once again settled down to try and live as a normal
family.

One thing that greatly helped us over this difficult period was the fact that Redbridge residents were at last beginning to stir. The combined effects of the council's house-wrecking policies and the evictions resulted in a Woodford housewife, Mrs Maureen Mistry, forming a Ratepayers' Protest Group to campaign for the use of empty houses in the central Ilford area and an end to illegal evictions. Mrs Mistry and her brother-in-law, Mr Brian Stevens, became very active in collecting signatures for a petition calling for the utilization of the empty houses. Mr Stevens, in particular, nagged the council members, and showed he was not a man to be fobbed off. He and Mr Richard Hoskins, the prospective Liberal candidate for Wanstead and Woodford (part of Redbridge) then conceived the idea of a trust to administer the empty houses. Not only did they offer to organize the utilization of houses that would become empty in the future, they also offered to repair the wrecked houses free of charge. Such a respectable idea from obviously responsible ratepayers was nevertheless rejected by the council and their refusal of this offer only served to isolate them still further.

Meanwhile another organization was formed to campaign for the reopening of the empty houses. This was called appropriately the Ad Hoc Committee for the Reopening of Empty Houses and consisted of representatives from the squatters, the Ratepayers Protest Group, Ilford Town Centre Residents Association, the Liberal Party, the Communist Party, individual members of the Labour Party and various other people from the Borough of Redbridge. This committee organized lobbies, pickets and marches in Ilford and served to demonstrate to the council how opinion was hardening against them. The number of people involved in the campaign also increased in May and June and the hard core of militants became outnumbered by all kinds of other people. In particular the assistance given to the London Squatters Campaign at this crucial period by Mr John Singleton and the Goodmayes Young People's Methodist Group is worthy of mention.

At the beginning of June we produced another pamphlet entitled *Evicted* attacking the methods of both the council and Quartermain. This was in fact a much more detailed version of

our earlier shorter pamphlet. *Evicted* was forty-six foolscap
pages long, and included nineteen sworn statements document-
ing our claims that both the evictions and the attitude of the
Redbridge Welfare Department were brutal and inhuman – an
impressive accumulation of evidence. This was our *pièce de
résistance* and we even organized a press conference to launch
it. We hoped for a mention of the pamphlet in the national
press, but the twenty column-inch write-up on page 3 of *The
Times* of 14 June, which included an address from which
people could obtain the pamphlet, exceeded our wildest expec-
tations.

The beginning of June also saw another pressure group of
Redbridge residents develop. This was started by Sam and
Doris Bornstein, a middle-aged couple who had been active in
the Labour Party for years. They sought to persuade ratepayers to deduct £1 from their rates in protest against their
money being spent on wrecking houses and hiring bailiffs. As
with all the other resident's groups this was important additional pressure on the council who, by now, were fast becoming more and more isolated.

A further act by the council served only to increase this
public disapproval of their policies. Towards the end of May,
LEB and Water Board workmen started digging up the road
outside all the wrecked houses and disconnecting these services
from the mains. I have already explained that the council,
when they had first started their house-wrecking policy had
ripped out pipes and cables. Our repairing of 26 Britannia
Road and the skill shown by our workmen in reconnecting
services must have led the council to take this extreme step of
cutting off the services at the mains. More ratepayers' money
was thus wasted, which displeased more residents. Also the
Town Centre Residents Association were particularly concerned at this, as every step to destroy the houses further
devastated the area, and pre-empted the result of the future
public inquiry into the redevelopment plan.

Their policy of cutting off services at the mains, however, did
have one good result for the council – it foiled a very ambi-
tious plan that we had embarked on. Briefly, this was that over
the weekend of 31 May to 1 June we were going to bring 150

volunteers to Redbridge to repair all thirty wrecked houses and install thirty families in them. Every squatting group in London was going to help. We had planned a shift system of workers for each house for that weekend. Cutting off the services at the mains really presented an obstacle – as it is not practical to install a family in a house with no services. We were so determined, though, that we even thought up ways of running pipes and cables from other houses and I am convinced, that, but for the expense, we could and would have done this. As it was, though, the plan did not materialize.

We had now overcome the setback to our morale that 21 April had caused and were now keen and ready to occupy and repair another council house and so push the council a little bit further. An attempt to do this on Saturday 14 June proved unsuccessful – the house we had in mind was so badly wrecked that even our volunteers shuddered at the amount of work and time it would take to repair it. However, we did manage to occupy an undamaged house in Oakfield Road that day. The house was locked up, and we were looking for a way in, which would not entail using force. Neighbours and police were watching us carefully. In the front garden of the house we spotted a round iron lid to the coal cellar. It was just large enough for a child to squeeze through and one of Danny McNally's kids climbed down into the cellar and emerged from the front door grinning. In we went triumphant. On Monday 16 June the council told us that they intended to use the house for a family on their housing list. As it was not our policy to occupy houses that the council intended to use, we discussed what we should do. The council, however, were not prepared to wait, and on the evening of 16 June bailiff George Green and his assistant arrived and we were peacefully ejected from the premises, a process we did not resist. The importance of this was that it demonstrated quite clearly that the council would evict us from any house that we occupied. We knew then that we would have to arrange for a twenty-four-hour guard on any house we took over.

On Saturday 21 June we received a boost to our morale. It was a great day for the Squatters Campaign in Redbridge – as great as 21 April had been bad. The Ratepayers' Protest Group set up a stall opposite Ilford Station to collect signatures for their petition. The Bornsteins set up a stall in Ilford High Road to collect support for their rates refusal. We organised the selling of *Evicted* in the High Road – and sold no less than eighty, at 2/6d a time (many people gave us considerably more). Most important of all, though, a group of us walked up to 6 Woodlands Road armed with tools, occupied the house and set about the task of repairing it. We decided to repair the first floor first and worked on it all that day and some of the next. By the end of the weekend we had made the upstairs quite habitable, having relaid the floorboards, replaced the windows and joined up the cut water pipes to fix up the sanitary facilities. Fortunately the Water Board had not cut off the supply at the mains. We knew that the council would probably try to repossess the house very quickly, so we made no attempt to repair the broken staircase at that point. We publicly stated, however, that our aim was to repair the house and when it was completed, either to move in a family ourselves or offer it to the council if they would guarantee to do so.

While we were repairing 6 Woodlands Road we ran short of floorboards, so some of our 'workmen' took some from another wrecked house, 21 Oakfield Road. On Sunday 22 June myself and Jim Nash went to look over that house and were caught on the premises. Some interesting charges were levelled against us. We were charged on three counts under the 1968 Theft Act: simple theft of wood (Section 1); entering a house and stealing wood (burglary, Section 9); and entering a house to do unlawful damage (Section 9). On 6 January 1970 we were acquitted of all three charges at North-East London Quarter Sessions. On the first two the judge directed the jury to return a verdict of not guilty; he ruled that in law moving wood from one council house to another does not constitute theft or burglary, as there was no intention permanently to deprive the owners of the wood. On the third (damage) charge the jury themselves acquitted us after hearing that we, in fact, were in the habit of *repairing* houses that the council damaged.

I have explained that our lesson of the previous week resulted in our being prepared to guard 6 Woodlands Road all the time. We had taken legal advice, and were determined to exercise our *legal rights* to defend it against attempts forcibly to evict us without a court order. On the morning of Monday 23 June Mr Patrick Walsh arrived and told us that the council would use force to evict us and we prepared for the attempt that we expected would take place within a couple of days.

However, 6 Woodlands Road was not to be where the council would make their next move. In the meantime the Fleming family had had to vacate 67 Oakfield Road as proceedings for possession were instituted by the owner in Ilford County Court. As it was not our policy to fight legal eviction at that time, the Flemings had been moved to 23 Audrey Road with Mrs McNeil which was anyway a much better house. (Mrs Garcia had decided to move to south London, and the South-East London Squatters installed her in a house in Lewisham.)

Redbridge Council seemed at this point suddenly to develop a great interest in the Flemings. A place in the council halfway home in Woodlands Road, Ilford – a much better place than the Grosvenor Road Hostel – was offered to them. Squatting is not easy, particularly when the family had had to move twice, as the Flemings had, and Chris Fleming seriously considered their offer. He had an appointment to visit the place at 3 p.m. on the afternoon of Monday 23 June. Here there is an odd coincidence. It will be remembered that the previous day Jim Nash and I had been arrested. A procedural hitch had prevented the police from charging us immediately, and we had been bailed to appear at Ilford Police station at precisely 3 p.m. on the 23rd.

At 3 p.m. on Monday 23 June, Jim and I duly presented ourselves at the police station, and we were kept hanging about for an hour. At 3 p.m., also, Chris Fleming kept his appointment with the Welfare Department in order to view the Woodlands Road halfway house. Something inside Chris told him that all was not right and, rather than go with the welfare officers, he ran out of the Welfare Department and all the way back to Audrey Road, where the only people in were his wife and children and two young girls who were visiting the house. Only a few minutes later, while Jim Nash and I were still at the police station, (and Chris should still have been with the welfare officials) another man kept rather a different appointment that afternoon, he knocked at the door of 23 Audrey Road. Chris Fleming opened it, and his visitor thrust a cane into his stomach, pushed him back into the back room, and barged in with half a dozen other people. As Chris was forced and pushed into the back room, too taken aback to say much, the man declared, 'I'm taking possession of this house – get out.' To Chris the face was familiar, but he was too shocked to think who it was. Mary Fleming, however, knew immediately. She saw the man and his cronies force Chris into the back room. 'That's Quartermain,' she cried, and broke down. The two visiting girls ran in fear from the house and tried to get help. Barrie Quartermain introduced himself and ordered everyone out, declaring that he was taking possession of the house. No, he told Mrs Pat McNeil who had arrived at the house, he hadn't got a court order, but then Barrie Quartermain does not always let that bother him. Panic and fright gripped the three women in the house, but a neighbour had phoned the police who arrived on the scene and asked Quartermain for a court order. Outside a group of council workmen with pickaxes were waiting to go in and smash up the interior of the house. A few press men also arrived at 23 Audrey Road.

This was the situation when Jim Nash and I arrived on the scene. In a situation like that the old proverb 'he who hesitates is lost', is very true. We had had legal advice that we could prevent these illegal evictions with force if necessary, and Jim and I intended to act on this without hesitation. On entering the house we discovered it full of the squatting families, two policemen and half a dozen 'bailiffs'. One policeman told me that they would not allow eviction to take place without a court order. Quartermain looked at me, glared and said, 'Right, I'm going to the Town Hall to get further instructions,' and to his men he said, 'You remain in the house until I get back.' Jim and I had no intention of allowing them to remain in the house and we asked the police to remove them. The police, who on this occasion, I must say, were very sympathetic, said they could not, so I declared that we would. 'Careful you don't lay yourselves open to assault charges,' said one police sergeant. 'Reasonable force is all we will use,' I replied, and with that Jim and I grabbed hold of the biggest bailiff and frogmarched him out of the house, down the path and off the premises. Three of his associates then followed him, after putting up only a little resistance.

We had cleared the house of bailiffs by the time Barrie Quartermain arrived back from the Town Hall. By that time the council workmen had gone, but we were all milling around in the street. Mr Quartermain walked up to us and said to Chris Fleming, 'I'm giving you until tomorrow to get out, otherwise I'll be back to get you out.' A row then ensued between Mr Quartermain and myself during which I noticed he was carrying a file entitled '23 Audrey Road – Eviction'. I wanted the names of the bailiffs concerned and as they had refused to supply them and I thought they might well be in the file, I took it from Mr Quartermain's hand. A fight broke out during which Barrie Quartermain broke my glasses and one of his men grabbed me round the neck. I wriggled free and hit back catching Quartermain in the eye while somebody else threw a bucket of water which soaked his suit and also Police Sergeant Tony Gooding's uniform. At this the police stepped in and stopped the fight and Mr Quartermain and his bailiffs made off, promising to be back.

As more squatters had arrived by this time, I made my way to 6 Woodlands Road and saw Mr Quartermain and his men there. Barrie had by now developed a large black eye following my punch. The house in Woodlands Road, however, was well defended and there were, in addition, no stairs. Realizing that he had no chance of success on that day, Mr Quartermain contented himself with sizing up the house and ordering us out – 'Or else I'll be back to get you out.'

This incident introduced a new intensity to the struggle in Redbridge. Just as our first two weeks in Ilford had been somewhat unreal, the three weeks following 23 June were even more so. We knew that Barrie Quartermain and his men would be back and we knew that for the sake of his public image he had to succeed next time. We had no intention, however, of vacating any houses without court orders being produced, merely because of his threats. Chris Fleming was also determined to resist any attempt at evicting him, and Mrs

McNeil felt the same. Any idea Chris might have had about accepting a place in the Woodlands Road halfway house was now gone.

We put out a general call for guards then, both out of a determination to resist and out of fear for our own bodily safety. On the evening of 23 June people began to arrive – all kinds of people, from extreme leftists to social workers and other people who disliked Quartermain's methods. About forty people met at 23 Audrey Road and a similar number met at 6 Woodlands Road. It was stressed that guards were needed for defensive purposes only and everyone assented. Hastily, barricades were prepared at both houses; 6 Woodlands Road, of course, was much easier to defend then 23 Audrey Road as we only occupied the first floor and there were no stairs.

A wide variety of tin helmets arrived for the 'defenders' to wear, and some people armed themselves with sticks to use if the bailiffs got in and set about people. Very late that night, or rather early in the morning of 24 June, both houses settled down to wait although very few people slept. I personally spent all night flitting from one house to the other while Jim Radford spent most of the time trying to organize the people in Audrey Road. At Woodlands Road Jim Nash and others organized the defences.

No one knew just when the bailiffs would arrive, so we resigned ourselves to the necessity of being on guard, back and front, all the time at both houses. At 4 a.m. a full television crew plus equipment arrived; it was our old friends from Thames Television's 'Today' programme – David Boardman, Alan Hargreaves & Co. All kinds of rumours started to circulate. Someone reported seeing Quartermain driving around in his car; an agency reporter said Quartermain was arriving at 7 a.m.; a *Daily Mirror* man said he had had a tip-off that Quartermain was on his way 'with a hundred men'. All the time we waited and watched.

Dawn came and went; morning proper descended on us, with people hurrying to work, including many of our guards. A skeleton force was however maintained in both houses. Still the bailiffs had not arrived but the daily papers had. The events of 23 June were covered extensively; most papers carried pictures either of bailiffs being removed from 23 Audrey Road, or of Barrie Quartermain's black eye. This was real news of course; everyone hates bailiffs and now, for the first time that anyone I spoke to could remember, they had actually been 'chucked out'. 'I'll be back, and they will be out,' said Mr Quartermain in almost every national paper.

Ever since we had arrived in Ilford we had had a good press. Our television coverage was also sympathetic. The eviction of 21 April and the publication of *Evicted* had only served to increase this. Redbridge Council had been complaining for months about the way the media had treated them, but if the news coverage of the earlier months had concerned the council, it was the last week in June and the first week in July that must have really upset them.

On Tuesday 24 June the bailiffs did not come, but just about everyone else did. Mr Patrick Walsh and Mr Findley came from the Town Hall to try to persuade Chris Fleming to go into a halfway house. When asked why the Flemings could not live in 6 Woodlands Road, the house we had repaired, they made no reply and seeing the 'Today' camera on them they beat a hasty retreat. An official from the Redbridge Welfare Department even had the nerve to put in an appearance, but was told to go away in no uncertain terms. One of our group, Tony Mahony, even brought the Bishop of Stepney, Trevor Huddleston, and Father Borelli, the Naples clergyman, to see the Flemings and McNeils. Attempts by these two to persuade Town Clerk Mr Nicholls to end the council's efforts at forcible eviction came to nothing. Similar arguments from Mr Robert Newland of the Town Centre Residents Association were also ignored. Even Mr George Henry Green, Redbridge Council's 'friendly bailiff' put in an appearance at Audrey Road – but only to see an elderly resident about non-payment of rates. Journalists from everywhere came and went all day, as did representatives from just about every left or radical organization in London – except, incidentally, International Socialism, who had a vaguely active Ilford branch but were now (and still are) politically opposed to squatting. To the neighbours in Audrey Road and Woodlands Road it was all quite unreal. 'I've never had so much fun since the blitz,' declared one:

others, I must admit, were not so friendly. All this was shown on 'Today' that evening, and Wednesday's national papers carried stories about the non-happenings of the day.

We in the houses of course could not relax, as we never knew when the bailiffs would arrive. We used that day to strengthen our defences and, when evening came, we settled down to another night of watching and waiting. Both houses allowed one journalist inside to try to capture the atmosphere for a story. As more supporters, whom we did not know, arrived we began a policy of vetting them, as we did not want 'agents provocateurs' in the houses, or people who had come to commit offensive violence. It was stressed repeatedly that the weapons and missiles we had accumulated in the houses were only to be used lawfully in defence of the houses against people trying forcibly to enter without the authority of the courts.

On the morning of Wednesday 25 June the bailiffs finally arrived. Everybody in the houses had expected a violent attack, but few had envisaged anything like what happened. At sometime around 5.30 a.m. more than a dozen men, dressed in steel helmets and goggles and carrying dustbin lid shields, ropes, ladders, crowbars and bricks, crept into Woodlands Road. Another half a dozen or so similarly dressed scaled the council garages at the rear of 6 Woodlands Road. Then shouting, waving their arms and throwing bricks and bottles they attacked. The initial onslaught drove the squatters back from the windows and the bailiffs seized their chance to get ladders up. Some more, led by the giant who had also participated in the 21 April evictions, smashed open the front door of the house and put a ladder up to the first floor and attempted to climb up.

Determined to defend the house and terrified for fear of what might happen to them if the bailiffs got in, the squatters in the house pulled themselves together and hit back. Ladders were pushed down; bailiffs were pushed back; helmets and shields and crowbars were 'confiscated'; water, paint, stones and bricks were thrown back at Barrie Quartermain and his men. Annoyed no doubt at having their initial onslaught repelled, and concerned for their public image, a fire was started

in one of the downstairs rooms and the whole house was filled
with smoke, but somehow the squatters kept control, hosing
water in the direction of the fire and throwing a large tarpaulin
down, and the bailiffs were repelled. At some point the Fire
Brigade arrived and eventually the police, who had stood
by and watched all this, intervened to end the battle.
The squatters, nine men and a girl, had held onto the house.
Quartermain had been defeated again, cheers and jeers were
hurled at the bailiffs as they retreated to prepare for their next
attack.

At Audrey Road, meanwhile, we had received warning that
the bailiffs were coming, and we prepared ourselves. Mary
Fleming and Pat McNeil were terrified of what might happen
to their children and they hurried out into a neighbour's house.
Chris Fleming joined them to comfort his wife, while the rest
of us waited apprehensively. Just before 6 a.m. Barrie Quartermain and his men arrived, this time without their helmets. 'Get
out before you get hurt,' shouted Barrie, but we declined his
'invitation'. At that the bailiffs entered the front gardens of the
houses opposite 23 Audrey Road and picked up bricks and
rocks and even empty milk bottles from the doorsteps, and
assembled in the middle of the road with their piles of missiles.
Some more of them went round to the back of the house. A
signal from Barrie Quartermain started the proceedings. The
'seven foot wonder' (as the particularly large bailiff had become
known) ran up the garden path and attempted to break the door
down. The rest of the bailiffs, including Mr Quartermain himself, picked up their bricks and bottles and hurled them at the
house, smashing almost every window. As at Woodlands Road
we were forced back by bricks and flying glass. Panic broke out
among some people and eventually we retaliated and threw
missiles back, successfully preventing the bailiffs from gaining
entry. By the time the police arrived it was nearly finished –
once again we had beaten back what the *Evening News* of 25
June was to call 'Barrie's tin-hat army'. Again, amid jeers and
taunts, the bailiffs retreated and this time left Ilford. We had
been completely victorious in the morning's battles, and Barrie
Quartermain had to content himself with threatening to 'be
back to do this lot', in order to save face. His self-confident

claim made in *The Sunday Times* just over a month earlier on 18 May that 'Councils who employ me don't have a Squatter problem anymore,' had turned somewhat sour.

Every edition of the evening papers on 25 June carried long accounts of the battles. 'Squatters Beat Barrie's Army (*Evening News* – early edition); 'Battle of Bailiffs versus Squatters' (*Evening Standard* – early edition); these were just some of the headlines. In addition an amazing picture of a band of helmeted men attacking the house in Woodlands Road was published. This picture, more than anything else, sums up the methods used by Quartermain and his men. Redbridge Council, of course, wanted to play the whole incident down but they had no chance. Their aggressive attitude with reporters only increased the degree of sympathy towards us, as we were willing to talk at any time. Every radio programme carried accounts of the battles and more and more journalists from all over the world poured into Ilford. The next day, 26 June, saw no respite for Redbridge Council. All the national papers, bar the *Daily Telegraph*, carried the story, and most printed the picture of the helmeted men hurling bricks at 6 Woodlands Road. Our friends from 'Today' were not to be left out; they interviewed Mr Quartermain on their programme on 26 June and his inability (naturally) to produce any sort of court authority for his actions did not exactly help the council's case. The attack on Redbridge Council continued on Friday 27 June, with feature articles in various papers. 'Private Eye with a Pickaxe Approach' was the headline in the *Daily Express*. 'Bailiffs and Brickbats' was the lead in the *Daily Mirror*'s Mirrorscope. 'Residents Support Squatters' blared the *Guardian* headline, while to add to it all BBC's 'Panorama' arrived on the scene and filmed a programme (which was not shown).

For us guarding the houses though there was no respite. Whether or when the bailiffs would return we had no idea, so we could not take chances. Our twenty-four-hour guard back and front at both houses had to continue. Although this was exhausting – by Friday 27 June many of us had literally only slept for an hour or two all week – it was also something we used to our advantage to maintain press interest. We were as keen to talk to pressmen as the council was to avoid them. We

even let some spend a night 'behind the barricades' to enable
them to write features. On the night of Thursday 26th – Friday
27th Adam Hopkins of *The Sunday Times*, an old friend of
mine from the Durham Buildings days and David Jenkins of
the *Evening Standard* joined us in Audrey Road. David Jenkins's article appeared in the *Evening Standard* on 27 June, hot
on the trail of the daily paper articles of that day already
referred to. 'Inside the Squatters Castle' it was called, and it
really was superb. Not to be outdone, Adam Hopkins's article
on 29 June was also very accurately written. The *Observer* of
the same day also published an article on the tense situation in
Ilford, just to add to the council's discomfort.

Meanwhile, the previous day, Saturday 28th, had seen
articles in *The Times* – 'Private Eye in the Public Eye' – the
Guardian and other daily papers. The *Guardian* article was
particularly interesting, as it showed that cracks were beginning to appear in the council's front. 'Bailiffs under Review'
was its heading and it included a (belated) statement from
former deputy Mayor, Mrs Lillian Fallaize, that she would
like to see the houses used for homeless people. The *Guardian*
of that day also published an amazing letter from Redbridge
Town Clerk, Mr Kenneth Nicholls. This said, referring to the
council's decision to act without court authority, that 'It is well
known ... that since last February the council have made four
attempts to enlist the aid of the courts, and it is on the experience thus gained that direct action ... is being taken.' Perhaps
even Redbridge Council had been influenced by the anarchist
ideals of some of the squatters. It was certainly interesting to
see the council advocating direct action. The *Evening News*
for Saturday 28th had also carried an important story, the
headline of which – 'Private Eye Barrie Calls a Halt' – speaks
for itself. Redbridge Council was beginning to shake.

Faced with all this, plus dozens of other news items and
reporters, including some from American press and radio,
Australian television, and the agencies, and also with leaders
in the national press – *Guardian* 26 June, the *Sun* 26 June,
Daily Sketch 26 June, *Evening Standard* 27 June – condemning them, Redbridge Council had to do something. On Monday 30 June a special joint meeting of the Town Centre Re-

development Committee and the Highways Committee, the two committees responsible for the redevelopment plan and thus the empty houses, was convened – all members of the council were invited and most attended. It was clearly a top-level meeting and the more intelligent of those present must have realised the dilemma which the council was in. They had tried the legal method of getting rid of squatters and this had failed, so they had taken to employing 'professional bailiffs' instead. At first this had been successful – on 21 April – and no doubt many councillors had breathed a sigh of relief; but now it had not only proved unsuccessful, it had completely back-fired on them. The name of Redbridge Council was fast becoming notorious, and every day saw more and more condemnation heaped on them from all quarters.

Some kind of offer had thus to be made by the council; the problem for the council was how to make it and save as much face as possible. Had the council made a conciliatory move as soon as we moved into Redbridge back in February, they could have come out of the affair quite well. But now, after a six-month struggle to open up the empty houses, after court battles and defeats for the council, after their house wrecking and after what were probably the most incredible street battles ever seen in Britain on this issue, almost any offer by the council would be seen as a climb-down; and yet they had to do something. Thus they made a statement – they were considering a policy change, they would review the whole situation regarding the empty houses in Ilford, they were even instructing the borough engineer to consider the cost of repairing the wrecked houses; at the same time, to save face, they had to reassert the policy of removing squatters by force. All this was what came out of the meeting of 30 June, but such was the public image of the council that even this backfired on them somewhat. Details of what had happened at the meeting reached the *Evening Standard* of 1 July. Many of the more intransigent councillors had obviously used this meeting to vent their spleen verbally, and their statements did not look very good in print. 'It's Total War Against the Squatters', was the headline in the *Evening Standard* on 1 July and the story went on to quote some more of the idiotic and brutal remarks made at the meeting, like one councillor saying, 'We should use tear gas on the swine.'

The morning papers for the following day, 2 July, were somewhat different, as by this time the council had had time to issue its press statement. 'Council Make Peace Offer' was the general tone of the reports, and although this may well have been rather humiliating for the council (as I have said *any* offer had to be at that stage) it was certainly preferable, I would think, to reports about 'tear gas' and 'total war'. I have already indicated that part of the council's offer involved a 'review' of their policy; it also gave us until Friday 4 July to vacate council property, or else bailiffs would again be sent to remove us. Unofficial sources had informed us that Barrie Quartermain had been sacked because of his bad public image (and no doubt his failure) and that a 'firm in the Midlands' were being talked about.

From our point of view we welcomed any suggestions that the council were going to change their policy regarding the empty houses, but we certainly had no intention of moving out or succumbing to threats of removal by 'a hundred men from the Midlands'. There were various reasons for this: first, of course, we had a responsibility to the families squatting and we had no intention of moving them out onto the streets; second, it was all very well for the council to talk of 'reviewing' its policy, but why should we trust the council in the light of its past record? There was no time limit on the review, so what was to stop the council spending months and months on it and then forgetting about it when things had quietened down. We had no guarantee that it would not go the same way as their previous offer of March 1969. So we strengthened our defences and prepared for another big attack on the two houses.

Both houses in fact became fortresses. Woodlands Road was the easier to defend as we occupied only the upstairs and had no families there yet. The most incredible defences were arranged, with pits and booby traps in the garden, and electric wiring in the loft should there be an attempt to enter through the roof. The Audrey Road house was equally fortified: the whole of the front and back garden became a mass of barbed wire; the only way in was through the front door which was narrow and therefore could easily be defended. At both houses we arranged a guard rota to keep watch twenty-four hours a day.

It was during this week that Chris Fleming became ill. Chris had developed epilepsy many years earlier while with the United Nations peace-keeping force in the Congo but at normal times he was only mildly affected by it. The extreme tension of living under siege conditions, with numerous guards always having to be present, finally affected Chris, and towards the end of that first week in July he started to behave oddly. He walked around as though drunk and on a number of occasions this resulted in his falling down the stairs. At that stage his epilepsy had not manifested itself but his condition gave us all cause for concern. Chris, however, was determined to see the struggle through to the bitter end and he flatly refused all offers to go away for a few days, and towards the end of that first week he seemed to improve considerably.

It was by Friday 4 July, the end of that week, that we were supposed to be out or else the 'hundred men from the Midlands' would be coming to remove us. Although we were in no way afraid of this, we were always prepared to discuss matters and we made representations to the local MP, Arnold Shaw, to initiate discussions between us and the council. Mr Shaw's sole contribution to the dispute, until that point, had been to bemoan the street battles and to suggest as a solution the passing of a law to make squatting illegal. (This is tantamount to blaming the victim of a vicious assault for putting his face in the way of the attacker's boot.) However, Mr Shaw did manage to arrange discussions. At the same time one of the Tory councillors, Leslie Hipkins, approached me to see if there was any possibility of talks ending the deadlock. I informed him that we were always ready to negotiate and he also set about arranging this.

The 'last minute talks' took place between myself and four council representatives – Alderman Harold Cowan, chairman of the Redevelopment Committee; Alderman Ray Dalton, leader of the council; Councillor Isaac Natzler, the new Mayor, and Mr Kenneth Nicholls, Town Clerk – at 4.30 p.m. on Friday 4 July. Arnold Shaw was also present. The talks

lasted for about an hour and a half and the council, in addition
to the 'review' to which it was already committed, offered us
the following terms if we would guarantee to stop squatting in
Ilford. First they would accept responsibility for the ultimate
rehousing of the Fleming and McNeil families. This was an
important concession, as it not only meant that negotiation
was possible – without this we could not of course abandon
these families – but it also meant that we had forced the council to accept responsibility for two families from outside the
borough without the normal five-year residential qualification
– an unprecedented occurrence. Second, pending the review,
the council undertook not to wreck any more houses.

I agreed to submit these proposals to the squatters at 6
Woodlands Road and 23 Audrey Road and to return to the
Town Hall at 9.30 p.m. that evening to let the council know
whether or not we agreed to their peace offer. I first took the
proposals to Woodlands Road where I recommended their
acceptance. I was not happy about them, for the reasons I have
indicated, but I was prepared to play the Devil's Advocate and,
anyway, I was worried about the effect of a further siege on
Chris Fleming's illness. To say that the Woodlands Road
people rejected the terms would be putting things mildly. I was
yelled and screamed at for even suggesting them; words like
'sell-out' and 'coward' were bandied about; I was called all the
names under the sun. One particular grievance was that I had
negotiated these terms by myself without any other squatters
being present. I accept that this was a very serious mistake on
my part and I should have taken at least one other person with
me. The intensity of the feeling, however, cannot be ascribed
solely to this: in fact over the previous few days a kind of
'house parochialism' had been developing at Woodlands Road
caused, I think, by the siege conditions plus the lack of any
family in the house which led the comrades to regard the
house as theirs. This took the form of people from the besieged houses no longer being considered simply as squatters,
but as 'someone from Audrey Road' to be opposed by 'a representative from Woodlands Road'.

The council's peace terms were thus entirely rejected by
Woodlands Road and, apart from the nagging worry about

Chris Fleming's illness, I was not upset at this, despite my Devil's Advocate role. I then took the proposals to Audrey Road where they were also rejected. Significantly, both the Flemings and Mrs McNeil were strongly against accepting them. As Chris Fleming said, 'We've no idea what the council mean when they say they accept "responsibility for ultimate re-housing". We could be left to rot in a hostel for years.' In addition to this I think the main reasons for the rejection of the proposals were that we had no guarantee that the 'review' would ever take place; we distrusted the council (not surprisingly), and also the actual time when the offer was made hardly helped matters. To make any offer with the threat of 'a hundred men from the Midlands' arriving next day is hardly conducive to proper consideration of the 'offer'.

At 9.30 p.m. that evening then, three people (I was not one of them) returned to the Town Hall to inform the council that we had rejected their offer, were not going to move out, and to challenge them now to bring in the bailiffs. At both houses we prepared to resist: word had gone out that we had until that day to be out and that the bailiffs were coming next day, so dozens of guards arrived. On the night of Friday 4 to Saturday 5 July both houses were packed and few people got any sleep. Everybody was very apprehensive; we had no definite knowledge which firm of bailiffs the council was going to employ, but we had a pretty good idea who it would be. There are very few firms that will either touch this kind of work or are capable of mounting such a large operation. Quartermain's Southern Provincial Investigations had already been knocked out. The other big firm, and one which was situated in the Midlands, is Midlands Counties Investigators.

At 4.30 a.m. the morning of Saturday 5 July one of our street guards rushed into 23 Audrey Road declaring that he had seen 'four army lorries full of men – over a hundred of them – arriving at the top of the road'. This was it we thought. We prepared to defend ourselves, terrified that if these men got on top of us we would be physically butchered. We waited, tense, determined, frightened. The tension was too much for one or two people; one man reported seeing 'the seven foot wonder' in the front garden (an impossibility as the whole garden was one mass of barbed wire). After a quarter of an hour's wait we sent out scouts. There was no sign of any men or any lorries. It had been a false alarm. There were no men and there was no attack that day. We calmed down somewhat, although complete relaxation was still not possible as we had to be prepared for an onslaught at any time.

It was over this weekend that Chris Fleming, who seemed to have improved a little, had a relapse and became very ill. This time his epilepsy started to manifest itself and Chris began having fits with increasing regularity. By Monday 7 July he was in a serious condition, but he steadfastly refused all suggestions that he should go away to rest or that he should go into hospital. On one occasion Chris had six epileptic fits in half an hour and we were extremely worried. At this point, on Monday 7 July, we decided in conjunction with Mary Fleming that Chris must not live behind barbed wire and barricades any longer and that evening we decided to take down the barricades at 23 Audrey Road. The problem was, of course, how were we to defend the house now? We decided to use Chris's illness to our advantage as much as possible.

Redbridge Council had tried both to reduce the amount of publicity the events were getting and to make it more favourable to them. They had had little success: journalists from all over the world, including *Izvestia* and Moscow Radio, were still visiting us and we were only too keen to talk to them. The British press also remained interested. On 1 July the *Daily Sketch* had run a sympathetic feature on the squatters and Audrey Road, while all the week articles had continued to appear including one in the *Guardian* on 4 July announcing that the previous day I had successfully (at last) taken out summonses against Barrie Quartermain and two of his men, charging them with riot. We were thus legally on the attack also. On Sunday 6 July *The Sunday Times* had followed up its story of the previous week with another entitled 'Minister Backs Squatters'. This referred to a government circular that had been sent out recommending local authorities to utilize empty houses. On the same day even the *Sunday Telegraph* carried an article entitled 'Ruthless Days at Redbridge', while the *Sunday Mirror*'s Broadside page took exception to a statement by Alderman Gleed, the former Mayor, that he would like to 'sweep (squatters) away with a mechanical brush'. On Monday 7 July the publicity continued in both the *Guardian* and *The Times*. The article in the latter was really excellent; it absolutely castigated the council. Its title will suffice to show its theme – 'Council Wrecking Houses but Redevelopment Scheme may not be Approved'. I think this article, more than any other, must have worried Redbridge Council as it questioned their whole redevelopment plan.

When, then, we took down the barricades at 23 Audrey Road we decided that our best defence was to make this as public as possible by using the continued press sympathy for our campaign. The papers for Tuesday 8 July thus proclaimed that we had removed the barricades from 23 Audrey Road, because of Chris Fleming's serious breakdown, and 'dared' the council to send in bailiffs. They were thus in another unenviable position; so much so that Alderman Cowan assured Mrs Doris Bornstein, who had by now become one of our most active supporters, that the council would not send in bailiffs as Chris was ill.

We were obviously on the verge of a major success, and all that was needed was a little bit more pressure on Redbridge Council. It was at this point that some of our comrades nearly managed to achieve defeat at the moment of victory.

6. Agreements at Redbridge

The people who made up the squatting group changed repeatedly. This was at once a good thing and a source of difficulty. It was good because it meant that a self-perpetuating élite never established itself. It was difficult because, in the nature of the case, secrecy was vital and the more new people appeared on the scene so the problems of security became more apparent.

There remained, however, a nucleus of people who had been involved from the very beginning – myself, Jim Radford, Alf Williams, Malcolm Conn, Trevor Jackles and others. Anyone could join us provided that they showed themselves willing to work and act sensibly. For example, after attending only one meeting, four members of the Ilford branch of the International Socialists who showed themselves to be keen were co-opted onto the various committees needed to arrange the squat. All four of these were to become leading lights in the campaign during the coming months and two of them, Alan Reid and Sally James (now married), remained involved for long after.

I have already mentioned briefly the split that had developed between Audrey Road and Woodlands Road. The next two or three weeks following the removal of the barricades at Audrey Road saw this develop and take on serious proportions. The state of siege that continued at Woodlands Road soon began to affect all those who had lived there more or less permanently for about three weeks. Apart from 6 Woodlands Road becoming their home and fortress, the fact that they had, of necessity, to live communally also caused it to become 'their' commune. They were by this time publishing a 'Squatters Report' which was circulated to the neighbours. In itself this was an excellent venture, of course, but unfortunately its very existence served only to knit together a small group of people who became increasingly hostile to all outsiders, except those who accepted their commune ideas.

Many of the newcomers to the squatting group had responded to our call for guards, as had many other people, but at Woodlands Road a small group of the worst type of 'anarchists'[1] gathered and thought they had established the free society at 'their' house. The interests of the squatting families became subordinate to 'the revolution'. The extent to which they were out of touch with reality can be seen from their attitude to the fact that we had forced the council to accept housing responsibility for the Flemings and McNeils. I have explained how vague this was and criticized it from this angle already; the Woodlands Road comrades, however, criticized it from a totally different standpoint. They considered it a sellout; they wanted a 'commune of Ilford residents' to accept responsibility for rehousing these families. Let me say right away that I entirely agree with the principle; but in Ilford, July 1969? It was not just a mistake; it was lunacy to talk in those terms.

The effects of the split were that Jim Radford, Tony Mahony, myself and others became 'baddies' and 'sellers-out' in the eyes of the communards. Worse, though, was the fact that virtually all they were prepared to do was build bigger and better defences at 6 Woodlands Road long after it had become clear that the 'threat' of a further attack by bailiffs was probably only a face-saver by Redbridge Council. The fact that Barrie Quartermain and two of his men were facing riot charges also lessened the possibility of the council being able to employ more bailiffs to launch an attack. After all, what firm would take on the job knowing that similar charges would be brought against them?

At this point our public image was very important. We had occupied a house in Albert Road – the centre one of three wrecked houses. We now declared our intention of repairing it in order to make it into a 'show house'. A considerable amount of work went into this. During these weeks in July we made

1. I am not condemning either the idea of anarchism or all anarchists – indeed, if I wanted a label I would describe myself as an anarchist.

three attempts to occupy more houses. We repaired the upstairs of 33 Audrey Road and, but for bad luck, could possibly
have moved a family in – unfortunately a water pipe burst
somewhere under the path. Like Woodlands Road, this house
had not yet had the water disconnected at the mains but the
Water Board, rather than dig up the path to mend the burst
pipe, dug up the road to cut it off. A further house was occupied and repaired in Lockwood Road by some men from the
Ford Shop Stewards Committee. The support of organized
workers was an extremely important new factor. This began
during July and included the District Committee of the AEF,
the Shop Stewards Committee from Kelloggs site in Coryton,
some stewards from Plesseys, a local factory and the active
help of the Ford workers.

At this point, I was very much in favour of moving the
Beresfords back into Ilford as they were very keen to squat
again and in fact were feeling left out of things back at Council
Buildings. I proposed doing this and argued that we should
state publicly that we were leaving them unguarded as a further demonstration to the council that they should offer us
further concessions. This idea, however, was not accepted. We
also decided to repair 6 Woodlands Road completely, as we
had said we would in June. The 'communards' agreed to this,
but never in fact carried out the decision, despite its being repeated on a number of occasions.

It was this that could have meant defeat. The sight of a
group of people 'communing' at Woodlands Road did not help
our public image. Furthermore an incident occurred which
could have been really catastrophic had it gained publicity.
One afternoon I was approached by a neighbour who had
previously been sympathetic but now wanted to lynch me.
When I discovered the reason I was not surprised: two people
from Woodlands Road had been firing marbles from a cata-
pult and had hit him and dented his car. Had that reached the
local press we would have been finished. It was exactly because
we had not behaved like this in the past that we had got such a
good press coverage. Because of things like this and also because they feared further street battles on their doorstep (and
this was not our fault) the residents of the area started to turn

against us. Previously, throughout our stay in Ilford, some had shown support and some opposition, but there was no general hostility. As is natural, opinion had varied from road to road – Woodlands Road and Lockwood Road being far more sympathetic than Audrey Road.

However, our continued occupation of houses and the help of the Ford workers gave the council nothing to be glad about and our case continued to advance. We were much helped by the arrival of 'World in Action', the most respected and feared programme of its kind – this was a further factor which helped us. They filmed extensively at Woodlands Road and around Ilford and planned a 'confrontation' on Granada Television on 21 July. This really was what we wanted and it was just what the council wanted to avoid. A tremendous row broke out in council circles over who was going to appear for them. At first no one would, but as this would have given us half an hour to ourselves, Councillor Nicholas Hurst threatened a public row if prevented from appearing and clearly someone had to. Alderman Cowan, however, refused and as he was the man responsible for the redevelopment plan, this annoyed many councillors. The internal row continued and it was not until a few hours before the programme went out that anyone knew for certain just who the council representatives were going to be.

While all this was going on the Ad Hoc Committee for the Reopening of Empty Houses held a picket at the Town Hall, a street corner meeting and a march round Ilford in which about a hundred people took part. On 15 July the council met and nearly 200 people marched to Redbridge Town Hall and completely filled the public gallery. At this meeting the council affirmed their intention of holding a 'review' of their policy for empty houses, but they also supported the eviction action taken on 25 June. The atmosphere in the public gallery was electric. As the meeting went on the tension mounted and it erupted when the Mayor announced that 200 Ilford residents had signed an anti-squatter protest. Mrs Bornstein jumped up and announced that 2,000 people had signed a petition calling for the opening of empty houses. At this the Mayor closed the meeting and ordered the public gallery to be cleared. The hundred or more people in the gallery had no intention of accepting this: many rushed into the council chamber, others jeered and booed, there was some violence too; when the police did get people outside there were attempts to block police vans leaving the council car park. In all there were twelve arrests and the next day we got a bad press. It was the first time the squatters had got 'out of hand' (there had been demonstrations at the Town Hall before, and even some arrests, but they had been only minor incidents) which, considering what we had put up with, is a remarkable record, but it still gave the council their first partially favourable press publicity.

'World in Action' on 21 July soon reversed this, however. Alderman Dalton, Councillor Escott, chairman of the Highways Committee, and Councillor Mrs Roberts, chairman of the Housing Committee, appeared for the council and Barrie Quartermain appeared with them. Mary Fleming, Jim Radford, Jim Nash and I appeared for the squatters. I think this programme went very well for us. The best moment came when Councillor Mrs Roberts said that 43 Cleveland Road had been demolished 'as it was too big for a family'! When Jim Radford pointed out that it certainly had not been too big for the Beresfords and their seven children, she replied that it was too large for them to heat! What an amazing statement from a housing chairman. It is the best excuse for overcrowding I have ever heard. At the end of the programme Mr F. MacCall from the Ministry of Housing was brought in and he confirmed that the ministry had sent out a circular recommending that councils either use empty houses themselves or give them to voluntary housing associations to use. As the programme faded out we had a picture of our interviewer, Michael Scott, asking the council to meet us for talks and them stalling and making excuse after excuse.

New talks were to come however and quite soon at that. In fact they took place on 24 July at Ilford Town Hall. The council's representatives were the same as at the previous talks. Our representatives were elected by a full meeting. I was one, Chris Fleming and Trevor Jenner were the others. Trevor had been around for some considerable time and had been a tireless worker doing the thousand and one jobs that needed doing. He had lived at Woodlands Road since we first took the house and had been one of its main repairers. Unlike most of the people there, however, he had not become completely dominated by the 'siege mentality': he remained realistic and did everything in his power to prevent the split from getting wider.

We met the council representatives at 5.30 p.m. on 24 July. After an hour's discussion a draft agreement was drawn up which we would submit to a squatters meeting the following day. In return for our promise to stop squatting in council property the council agreed, as before, to accept ultimate responsibility for rehousing the Flemings and McNeils and not to wreck any more houses pending their review. We were assured also that the review would be completed shortly and presented to the vacation council meeting in August. Further, the council agreed that the Flemings and McNeils could, if they wished, have first refusal on any properties to be used after the review. This was important as it would ensure that they were not left to rot in hostels for years. Finally the council agreed to meet us again after the review had been completed to explain their reasons for using or not using particular houses. We were assured that in the case of houses they decided not to use they would consider seriously any suggestions we might make. In a number of ways then the offer went considerably further than the previous one: in addition there was no threat of 'a hundred men from the Midlands'.

At a meeting of the East London Squatters (as we now called ourselves – we had changed our name from London Squatters when more groups began to form in other parts of London) on Friday 25 July we put the proposals and outlined our case for accepting them. I will not describe in detail the heated discussion that took place, suffice it to say that the agreement was regarded as a 'sell-out' by the Woodlands Road communards. We argued that the agreement gave us what we wanted and that if the council decided, even after the review, to continue to leave all their houses empty for years then this would clearly constitute a breach of the agreement, giving us the right to squat again in Redbridge. By withdrawing now, thus showing our goodwill, we put further pressure on the council. Sure, we agreed this was not a revolution, but it was realism.

Eventually the agreement was accepted by a majority of over two to one (most of those who voted against the agreement had only been active a short while). I met the Mayor of Redbridge, Councillor Isaac Natzler, and signed it at 1 p.m. on Saturday 26 July 1969.

'We won't accept it,' yelled the communards, 'It's a sell-out,' and with that they prepared to defend their commune against everyone, including us. We had, according to the agreement, to vacate 6 Woodlands Road by noon on 31 July, but communards threatened to ignore this. We had accepted the offer in order to pressurize the council but, if we had failed to honour it, the whole plan would have backfired. The problem was how to remove the occupants of 6 Woodlands Road without a fight, as all efforts at persuasion and reason were met with abuse. However the problem was solved more easily than any of us had expected. Chris Fleming, who was about to move into his new flat (which incidentally was very good) on Wednesday 30 July, was prevented by the council from doing so as the Woodlands Road communards had declared their intention of ignoring the agreement. He stormed round to Woodlands Road and told the occupants in no uncertain terms what he thought of them. Fortunately the more intransigent and unreasonable communards were not present and those that were there declared that they had been completely misled by the hard-liners into thinking that by remaining at 6 Woodlands Road they were actually protecting Chris Fleming. They agreed immediately that they should honour the agreement. When the hard-liners returned they were livid about this but by this time their commune had been de-fortified so there was little they could do.

At noon on Thursday 31 July we vacated 6 Woodlands Road; the Flemings and McNeils had already moved from Audrey Road into council accommodation. However the struggle against Redbridge Council was not over. We had intended to keep a watchful eye on the council to see that they honoured the agreement. If they failed to, either in word or in spirit (e.g. by saying, 'having reviewed our policy we are not going to alter it and we are still going to wreck the houses that we acquire') we were prepared to squat in Ilford again and with renewed vigour. The council must have known this and they must also have realized that to break the letter or spirit of an agreement signed by the Mayor would result in further press condemnation and even more sympathy for the squatters.

In August the vacation council meeting duly considered the completed review and formally ratified the agreement signed with the squatters. Actually there had been quite a row over the agreement prior to the council meeting. Some councillors took great exception to the part which bound the council to meet us after the review had been completed to explain their reasons for using or not using houses and listen to suggestions from us. 'Humiliating' they called it and went on to say that we were laughing over our victory while the council had agreed to put us in a position which made us akin to 'Government Inspectors' over their policies. In the end though they had no choice but to ratify the agreement; to have refused to do so would have placed the Mayor (and the council) in an impossible position.

What has happened in Redbridge following the review? One of the results is that any houses that the council acquire and which are not needed until the second stage of the redevelopment plan in 1976 (like 43 Cleveland Road) must be used for housing purposes. This was ensured when the Ministry of Housing stated that they would not give the council loan sanction to buy the houses unless they were so to be used. This, in addition to preventing the council from leaving houses empty, also ended another of their favourite habits – using houses for the second stage as 'temporary council offices'. Of houses acquired for the first stage of the plan – twenty-two in Queens Road and Ilford Lane were to be used for housing purposes – the rest will be used for welfare purposes, to relieve overcrowding in halfway houses (in other words homeless families will be housed in them rather than in halfway houses). One condition was added; the cost of repairs and redecoration may not exceed £100 per year of the remaining life of the house, with a ceiling of £300. Houses not falling into this category would not be used. In practice this has meant that some of the houses acquired were used while some were not. The council also decided not to allow the unused houses to be taken over by a housing association for fear that the association would not be able to rehouse the families when the council needed the houses for redevelopment. Finally the council decided that the wrecked houses would cost too much to repair – £1,200 to £1,500 each – and so could not be used. This did not surprise us as we did not really expect to see the council actually repairing houses it had destroyed.

Clearly we had forced the council to make considerable concessions and brought about a change of their policy for short-life property, which would affect many houses over the next few years. However, the struggle in Redbridge was by no means over; we still had the right under the agreement to meet the council to hear how the implementation of the review was proceeding, and this meeting took place at the beginning of October 1969, when Carl Rosen, Brian Stevens and I met the Mayor (Councillor Isaac Natzler), Alderman Cowan and Alderman Dalton, the leader of the council, with Town Clerk Mr Nicholls and the Borough Engineer, Mr Bryant, present.

We heard how a number of houses the council had acquired had been surveyed and how some were being repaired ready for use. Others were already in use. However most of the discussion centred around those houses that the council were not going to use because they would cost too much to repair. We argued strongly that, although there might be some valid reasons why the council could not use them, there were no reasons why a housing association should not be offered them. As I have said the council had decided against this policy in August, on the advice of the Housing Manager, Mr David Perry. We pointed out that perfectly workable arrangements had been reached in many other boroughs, and stressed that Redbridge should follow suit. The council replied that if we could provide them with evidence of this and give them more details, they would be prepared to reconsider their policy. We agreed to do this, and the meeting ended.

Because many of the East London Squatters became pre-occupied with struggles which had subsequently developed in

Arbour Square, Stepney[1] and in Lewisham,[2] we delayed somewhat in presenting the council with the information about housing associations. I feel also that considerable blame for the delay must also fall on local people: we had created a climate where the council could no longer refuse to listen to them, and yet none of them pursued this matter. However, in June 1970, I finally drew up some detailed proposals for the use of those houses in the Ilford central area that were still being left empty. By this time I could not only point to arrangements other councils had come to with housing associations but also to the success of the Lewisham Council—Lewisham Family Squatting Association deal.[3]

This document was considered by the four relevant committees and, finally, on 15 July 1970 the council met and agreed to open negotiations about housing associations using short-life property. To quote the council minutes, they agreed to discuss the matter with

1. the Organisation proposed to be set up by Mr Ron Bailey (i.e. a squatting group on the Lewisham model) 2. Lend-a-Hand,[4] and 3. Shelter.

This decision, therefore, though a major step forward, allowed the council plenty of room for manoeuvre. Many people, myself included, suspected that the council would try to prolong negotiations over as long a period as possible. An effective way in which they could do this would be to play the three groups mentioned against one another, and discuss the matter separately with each, thus taking months finally to decide. The best way to prevent this, it seemed to me, was for all three organizations to form themselves into one and go to the council in a single local group. With this in mind I called a public meeting at Gants Hill Library on 23 July and invited many people from the borough. This meeting was well attended by a wide variety of local people including members of the squatters, Town Centre Residents Association, Shelter, and also Mr Robb Spencer of Lend-a-Hand. The need for unity was stressed and in particular Robert Newland of the Town

1. See p. 143.
2. See p. 132.
3. See p. 135.
4. A local housing association.

Centre Residents Association pointed out that, although the
council had agreed to negotiate, they were also still demolishing houses in advance of the proposed redevelopment of central Ilford. Thus, the longer negotiations went on, the more
houses would be demolished. It was a good meeting; a unity
was created and a new group formed – The Redbridge Community Housing Action Group.

In July 1970 the group met the council. On our side there
were James Alexander who was secretary of the Trinity Housing Association, and who had joined us at the meeting, Reg
Dale of Lend-a-Hand, deputizing for Robb Spencer, Pleasie
Mills from Shelter, and myself. For the council there were Mr
Perry, Housing Manager, and Mr Bryant, Borough Engineer.
The implementation of the plan was discussed, and we submitted a list of the houses we wanted. We left the meeting
fully expecting the matter to be approved by the next full meeting of Redbridge Council, in September 1970.

It was not: but the council cannot be blamed entirely for
this. Robb Spencer of Lend-a-Hand, a committee member of
the Redbridge Community Housing Action Group, broke our
unity. He applied for the houses on behalf of Lend-a-Hand
(despite the fact that he had already done so by virtue of his
being on the committee of the new group). Worse still, however, he launched an entirely irrational press attack on the
squatters and 'irresponsible' people and urged the council only
to deal with 'responsible' groups like Lend-a-Hand. Had the
council wanted the opportunity to delay they could not have
hoped for a better one. The September council meeting could
not consider the matter, as negotiations with Robb Spencer
were still going on. In addition, how could the Redbridge
Community Housing Action Group put pressure on the council to hurry things up when one of its own committee members
had denounced it as being irresponsible and urged them to deal
only with another group.

In the weeks following, pressure was exerted on Robb
Spencer to withdraw his approach to the council and maintain
the united front. Despite the fact that this was successful the
damage had been done. The matter was delayed for months
and it was not until February 1971 that Redbridge Council

finally agreed to hand over short-life houses for use for home-less families by a housing association. Fortunately the housing association that got them was James Alexander's Trinity Housing Association, and so, some seven months after my de-tailed proposals, the council had finally reversed its refusal to deal with voluntary bodies. By that time more houses had been demolished in advance of the proposed redevelopment plan (still not approved by the Minister). Robb Spencer had given the council a chance to delay and they had used it to the full.

Perhaps the real lunacy and inhumanity of Redbridge Coun-cil's whole policy for short-life houses is the fact that Trinity Housing Association was given four houses that the council had previously wrecked during the squatters campaign back in the early months of 1969.

Although Redbridge Council had been defeated over their empty houses policy, I still felt that a further push was needed to persuade the council to hand more houses over to voluntary bodies. Therefore in June 1971 I once again met council officials and argued that, although we supported their handing houses to Trinity Housing Association, there were still some that that association did not want to use, and that we wanted to occupy them. Tentative arrangements were made for me to see if we could use some in Ley Street, Ilford, but then on 1 July 1971 the final bombshell hit Redbridge Council, who, by this time, must already have been pretty fed up with the years of pressure and protest about both empty houses and the re-development plan itself. The final blow however was one that really rubbed salt into their wounds – the Secretary of State for the Environment announced that after considering the objec-tions to the central Ilford redevelopment plan, he agreed with them. He therefore rejected the plan completely and refused to grant the compulsory purchase orders issued by the council.

For the previous four years the council had waged a losing battle to leave houses empty, wrecking them, and demolishing them in advance of the plan. But in July 1971 the Secretary of State had turned down the plan. Two Redbridge residents im-mediately objected to the District Auditor about the waste of ratepayers' money by the council. In Redbridge Town Hall there was chaos and confusion, and the matter of the empty houses again stuck out like a sore thumb. Many houses recently acquired had been boarded up as they only had a life expectancy of a few months, but the rejection of the scheme altered this drastically. 'We are open to suggestions,' announced the council, some four years after they should have done. The result was that the council used some of the houses for their own housing purposes, and Trinity and other housing associations were given the rest, together with Redbridge Council loans to repair them.

I mention this rejection of the plan not because it has anything to do with squatting now, but because it is one further justification for the squatters' first move into Redbridge, the one aim of which was to stop a council leaving good houses empty for a scheme that had not been approved by the Ministry – and in the final analysis was not approved.

To return to matters more directly related to the Redbridge squatting campaign I will finish this account by describing the eventual outcome of our legal battle against the bailiffs. Following the attempted eviction at 23 Audrey Road on 25 June 1969 I had commenced proceedings against Barrie Quartermain and Brian Morley for riotous assembly. I subsequently added threatening behaviour under the Public Order Act in case the charge of full riot was not proved. After a heated committal hearing lasting six and a half days both Quartermain and Morley were committed to the Old Bailey on both charges. At this point the Director of Public Prosecutions took over the case, which was finally heard at the Central Criminal Court on 2 December 1970, and numerous witnesses were prepared for a long hearing which did not materialize. A deal had been arranged: Quartermain and Morley pleaded guilty to causing an affray, and in return the riot and threatening behaviour charges were dropped. The Judge, Mr Justice Edward Clarke, QC, bound both of them over for two years and awarded some costs against them. One can only wonder what kind of sentence they would have got if they had been associated with a left-wing group!

However, the point had been established and that was the most important thing. The Quartermain evictions were illegal

– as we had said, in the face of official scepticism, all along. Court orders *are* needed to evict even squatters. We had won the legal argument too.

But perhaps the biggest triumph of all came in the spring of 1972. Although Trinity Housing Association and the council were by this time using many empty houses there were still some that they did not plan to use.

These houses were handed to the squatters – including 6 Woodlands Road – almost three years after the violent battles of 1969.

7. The Spread of the Movement

A number of short-lived campaigns came into being. They were important, less for the growth of organizations elsewhere than for the lessons that they taught. They were also, of course, an indication that squatting could grow into something really big. Detailed history of these campaigns can add little to the understanding of the movement so I shall content myself with highlighting those which we found instructive.

Notting Hill is, of course, a notorious area for bad housing – the more so because it is part of one of the richest boroughs in England, the Royal Borough of Kensington and Chelsea. The squatting group formed in that borough began with a demonstration squat in a block of luxury flats in order to publicize the plight of the homeless. They repeated the tactic in January 1969 by occupying a £17,000 'town house'. It was not only publicity that they gained by these moves, but also valuable experience in organization. Later in the same month, before even the East London Squatters had been able to squat their first family, the group installed a family, Mrs Maggie O'Shannon and her two children, in an empty house. The fight surrounding this squat occupied the national headlines for days and went on with some publicity for weeks. Eventually in March the Notting Hill group moved again and squatted two more families – without much success but watched by both press and television. Later in 1969 the borough council sought to sell two houses to property speculators – the Notting Hill Squatters attended the auction and completely disrupted the affair by bidding outrageously high for the houses. This resulted in a protest being published by the *Guardian* 'at the council's policy of selling requisitioned properties when there are over 4,000 people on the housing waiting list'.

In Leeds another group occupied an office block in the city

centre using grappling irons to gain access to the balcony roof. In both these cases the value of publicity was demonstrated. Because the press and television became so interested it was not possible for the authorities simply to shrug the incidents off.

Notting Hill's exploits were also the result of very careful planning and organization. The value of this was further demonstrated in Surrey where the lack of it resulted in disaster. Because the Surrey squatting group was ill-organized the family that they installed in an empty house was evicted within two days and the group collapsed.

Probably the most obvious lesson to be learnt is that any group that comes into being must, as soon as possible, get a family into a house. The north London group in Harringay did just this and, although the council employed Quartermain and his men to get them out, they were shamed into rehousing the family and into using other empty houses at their disposal.

There are four other areas, however, where more protected squatting campaigns have occurred. One of course is east London, where there is still considerable activity. The others are south London, Brighton and south-east London. From all these campaigns there are important lessons to be learnt, so I will examine them in some detail.

In south London the squatters group was formed in March 1969 by a collection of anarchists, International Socialists (who later dropped out) and people interested in housing who were not politically committed.

Their first demonstration was on 29 March when they occupied, for a day, a five-storey office block in Brixton which had been empty for three years. The group then embarked on a comprehensive survey of empty property, hostels for the homeless and halfway houses in their area. They were centred mainly around Battersea and in the London Borough of Wandsworth generally. Their particular interest, as far as empty houses were concerned, was the Home Road development area of Battersea – the place that had attracted the attention of the Durham Buildings Tenants Association back in November 1968 and over which the local Liberals had run a press campaign in an effort to get the empty houses used.

Not only had the Liberals failed but certain sections of the redevelopment plan had been scrapped too. The Wandsworth Council thus had many empty houses on its hands and rather than use them for families on the waiting list or for families in local hostels the council decided to sell them. The Home Road area of Battersea was thus an excellent target for a squat: as in Redbridge, conventional means had been tried in an effort to persuade the council to use the houses. In addition, Battersea Bridge Buildings, an old decrepit tenement block used as a halfway house, was nearby and the South London Squatters canvassed the families there.

Mrs Pat Smith, who had five children and had spent the last seven years in hostels, was the first from Battersea Bridge Buildings to decide to squat. In the middle of April the South London Squatters planned to move her into an empty council house but this proved unnecessary. The mere threat was enough to achieve what the previous seven years had failed to achieve: the local council suddenly decided to give Pat and her family a council house. The South London Squatters thus started with a victory and clearly, I think, the long campaign in Redbridge was beginning to worry other authorities, who were keen to avoid a similar situation if they could.

The south London group quickly followed this up on 26 April by squatting two more families, the Sheppards and the Fosters, both from Battersea Bridge Buildings, in 17 and 19 Bullen Street, SW11. On the same day Councillor Denis Mallam, chairman of the Wandsworth Housing Committee, met members of the squatters group. He was obviously out to avoid a Redbridge-style confrontation (five days earlier the first Redbridge Council–Quartermain evictions had taken place) and also out, as he himself put it, to 'save face'. He was worried that the families were not Wandsworth families (Battersea Bridge Buildings is administered by the Welfare Department of the London Borough of Hammersmith) and he was also determined that the families could not stay in 17 and 19 Bullen Street, as they were both to be sold to the London Housing Trust. But he did want to avoid a confrontation, so he proposed a deal. The families could occupy two other empty properties in Wandsworth, provided that the squatters could persuade one of the many housing charities to accept the responsibility for administering them.

Clearly, if this could be arranged, it would be a reasonable compromise: the council would have avoided another 'Redbridge' and the families would have been rehoused. From the point of view of the wider aims of the squatters movement it would also have been advantageous – the message to other homeless families in the area would have been clear – squat and you get a decent house. This is exactly the kind of situation that Jim Radford is expert at handling. However the south London group were divided on the issue. While some recognized what I consider to be the obvious advantages of such a solution – the message to other badly housed families that squatting works – others favoured a confrontation with the council. The result was that the Sheppards were rehoused by a charity, but completely out of the district, while Joan Foster remained in Bullen Street.

The council, while wishing behind the scenes to find a settlement had, on the surface, to save face. A High Court possession order was obtained against Mrs Foster who, however, remained determined to 'squat on' and not to go back to Battersea Bridge Buildings. It was then decided to re-squat Mrs Foster in another house, this time in the borough responsible for her, Hammersmith. On 13 May Mrs Foster and her family moved into 22 Rumbold Road, Fulham, an empty Hammersmith Council house and immediately sent a letter to the council offering to pay rent and rates. There was considerable local support for Mrs Foster, as many families living in poor housing were annoyed at the council's policy of selling houses as they became vacant. 22 Rumbold Road was an excellent location for the squat as it was right next door to the house of Ernest Rodker, one of the leading activists in the Hammersmith and Fulham Squatters, with whom the south London group had now merged. Ernest is a militant of long standing: he is a member of the Wandsworth Community Workshop and had helped in the Durham Buildings struggle back in autumn 1968. A twenty-four hour guard on the house was thus easily mounted.

The move received publicity in both local and national press.

This was helped by a visit to the Fosters on 14 May from Bernadette Devlin, and shortly afterwards Liberal leader Jeremy Thorpe also turned up. Hammersmith Council however were not so interested in friendly visits. On the day of the squat Alderman William Smith, leader of the council, announced that the council would take 'all legal means to regain possession'. Mrs Foster said, however, that she was 'determined to stay'. Another Redbridge seemed to be brewing, particularly as the council flatly refused to discuss Mrs Foster's case with a housing society.

Nevertheless, at that stage the council restricted its 'hard line' to legal attempts to remove the squatters. At the end of May a High Court injunction was served on Mrs Foster ordering her not to continue her trespass, pending the council's application for possession of the premises. The squatters responded partly by ignoring the injunction and partly by conducting a publicity campaign against the council. Ignoring the injunction had its interesting side: the council could have sought to have Mrs Foster committed to prison for contempt of court. That they did not do so suggests that they realized that this would not redound to their credit. This idea is borne out by the action of the Tower Hamlets Council at the end of 1969 and Southwark Council in 1971 in failing to enforce injunctions (see pages 145–61, 170). Perhaps we may conclude that it is unnecessary for squatters to avoid them.

A council meeting was picketed and interrupted; Mrs Foster's case was presented at a public meeting organized by the council to discuss the future of the borough; a 'Street Fayre' was arranged in Rumbold Road. The result was that considerable local support was obtained for Joan Foster and the squatters. The Chelsea Labour Party passed a resolution deploring the council's 'waste of empty property', and on 19 June the *West London Observer* carried an open incitement from Mr George Simpson, chairman of Hammersmith Housing Committee, to the 4,000 people on the council's housing list to 'band together and take over all types of empty property'. Hammersmith Council replied to this the next day, 20 June, by obtaining a High Court (temporary) injunction restraining Mr Simpson from inciting people to trespass, and on 24 June Mr

Simpson gave the court a permanent undertaking not to do this.

It was at the height of all this that the Hammersmith and Fulham Squatters decided to strike again. On 1 July Mrs Grace Craig and her family were installed in 39 Moore Park Road. Mrs Craig had previously been living in a small basement flat in West Kensington, which was damp, affected by dry rot and had plaster falling from the walls. This squat, however, ended very badly: only two days later the council bailiff arrived and finding only one guard at the house, and also finding a basement door open, so enabling him to enter without using force, he evicted Mrs Craig, who was taken by the squatters group to join Mrs Foster at Rumbold Road.

On the face of it this eviction would seem to have reversed the trend that we had managed to establish – no forcible evictions without a court order. The eviction of Mrs Craig was perhaps a little surprising, but was it illegal? Was Hammersmith Council reversing the precedents we had managed to establish? On the former point I think that it was probably of dubious legality – the bailiff apparently did push one guard out of his way which, in law, amounts to force. On the other hand it seems that he entered the house by means of an open door. Entry through an unlocked door does not constitute forcible entry, nor does entry by means of a trick. It seems that while the guard was in front of the house the bailiff went round to the back. The entry by the bailiff was probably not forcible in strictly legal terms, or if it was then only technically so. Certainly there was nothing on the Redbridge scale (either 21 April or 25 June) so the council was not publicly pilloried. There is a qualitative difference between a council acting illegally and violently in evicting a family, and thus bringing untold trouble onto their own shoulders and widespread support for the squatters, and in one council bailiff tricking his way into a house and turning a family out with little publicity. For this reason I do not think – and all subsequent events prove this – that the eviction in Moore Park Road on 3 July was a serious reversal for the squatters campaign.

For the Hammersmith and Fulham Squatters, of course, it was a serious blow but, as I have said, Mrs Craig was taken to

Rumbold Road to carry on squatting. The council on the other hand was still as determined as ever to remove Mrs Foster, but they acted strictly according to the law. Shortly after Mrs Craig had joined her, the council's application for possession of 22 Rumbold Road was heard in the High Court – and granted; Mrs Foster was given until 30 July to 'deliver up possession' of the house.

It was at this point that the Fulham squatters again faced a decision – confrontation or evasion? They chose confrontation: the court bailiffs and police were to be fought. Mrs Foster would not be switched. In the words of the squatters themselves 'impregnable barricades had been built to defend Mrs Foster against any and all attempts to evict'. This was the situation at the end of July – and as eviction time approached Mrs Craig moved out, somewhat reluctantly, leaving the squatters and Mrs Foster to fight the bailiffs.

The fight never came. At the eleventh hour the Catholic Housing Aid Society stepped in and offered Joan Foster a house, which she readily accepted, and so she vacated 22 Rumbold Road. Had the squat been abandoned at that point then the Fulham squatters would have been able to claim a partial victory – the message to other local homeless families would have been clear: Joan Foster squatted and Joan Foster got a house – her first for seven years. Unfortunately some members of the Fulham squatters did not see things quite like this: they remained in 22 Rumbold Road, barricaded to the hilt and armed to the teeth. They were the same people who had been involved in the saga of 6 Woodlands Road in Ilford and after we had got rid of them at the end of July, they all moved to 22 Rumbold Road. That house now became their 'commune', their little bit of 'free England' to be defended at all costs against the 'capitalist-imperialist-fascist bailiffs and police'. 'Siege mentality' became absolutely predominant despite the entreaties of more sensible members of the group like Ernest Rodker living next door. The fact that there were no homeless families living there made no difference to the 'defenders' – the house had to be defended against bailiffs and sell-outs.

This situation continued until 22 September. It is true that at the beginning of September the communards did manage to get a family to join them, they used them to point to their critics and say, 'Look, we have got a family,' but by this time the damage had been done: this was a 'commune', in which families might well be given sanctuary, but it was not a family's home where guards were only required to stop an illegal eviction.

On 22 September the family that had moved in was persuaded to move out again by the Welfare Department, the police sealed off the road and, acting as bailiffs under the instruction of Mr A. Black, deputy Sheriff of Greater London, executed the High Court possession order obtained two months earlier, and evicted the occupants. The squatters campaign in Hammersmith however had certainly exerted considerable pressure on the council: they declared their intention to use the house themselves and have now installed a homeless family in it. That evening and the next day the squatters campaign received the worst possible publicity (if one excludes the activisits of the London Street Commune – a completely separate movement). The *Guardian* on 23 September proclaimed, 'Police Eject Squatters in "Armoury" '. Other papers carried similar headlines and stories. As a result of all this six members of the Fulham squatters were charged and subsequently found guilty of conspiracy to commit actual bodily harm to persons attempting lawful entry. They received suspended prison sentences – after having spent many months in prison awaiting trial.

It is worth considering whether the eviction at Rumbold Road was lawful. The Fulham squatters argued that, as Mrs Foster had left, the possession order was no longer valid. However, the order concerning Rumbold Road instructed Mrs Foster and her agents and servants to vacate the house. Clearly this did not happen – the 'agents and servants' remained in possession in breach of the court order. At 43 Cleveland Road a similar order existed – but was obeyed. The Beresfords moved out, the house was emptied and another family moved in. In addition it is also important to note that a High Court writ is different from a County Court writ. Redbridge obtained the latter against the Beresfords, 'in personam', ordering them individually to do something, whereas Hammersmith Council obtained a High Court writ under Order 45 Rule 3 which simply orders the Sheriff to take possession of the premises. Thus the Redbridge eviction was illegal and that is why Quartermain was employed. Clearly there is a considerable difference between the two cases. A technicality this may be – but an important one nevertheless. The whole process by which we, in the squatters movement, have frustrated the law is based on technicalities. At Rumbold Road the authorities used one that the squatters had left open. Our only defence is to sew them up so tightly by steering a careful course through the technicalities of the law that this is not possible.

The Rumbold Road eviction was well timed by the authorities, it came when the anti-'squatter' hysteria generated by the London Street Commune was at its height. Any excuse to act against squatters was seized on – with public approval. The Fulham 'armoury' was just what the authorities needed.

The South London Squatters group thus declined. However some of its members were soon to assist in the Victoria Dwellings Action Committee. This was a group that waged a partially successful campaign throughout 1970 against Wandsworth Council's intention of closing Durham Buildings as its welfare accommodation and instead using Victoria Dwellings – a similar type of old tenement block. The action committee, while agreeing with the closure of Durham Buildings, argued that homeless families should be accommodated in empty property in the borough. The campaign attracted widespread local publicity and support and was successful in reducing the number of families put into Victoria Dwellings and in pressurizing the council to use more short-life property. Later, at the end of the year, some members of the group formed themselves into a Lewisham type squatting group and approached the council demanding to be allowed to use short-life property in the borough along the lines arranged in Lewisham.

Outside London the longest and most determined squatting campaign took place in Brighton. The chief mover in the formation of the Brighton Squatters group was Andy Wright who, after spending a week with us in Ilford at the beginning of May 1969, returned to Brighton determined to start a squatters group there. He was immediately successful and within two weeks the newly formed Brighton Squatters were holding their first token demonstration. The formation of the Brighton Squatters was greatly helped by the fact that there was already a campaign in existence in the town based on the question of housing. This was organized by the Brighton Rents Project, an alliance of socialists, Labour Party supporters and housing militants of all kinds. They had gathered and publicized information concerning bad housing in the town, campaigned to inform tenants of their legal rights and collected a petition with 2,000 signatures demanding 'Homes for people not profit'. Of all the southern seaside towns Brighton has the largest working-class population and the worst housing conditions.

On the weekend of 10 May 1969 the group staged its first token squat at two empty houses owned by the council in North Place. This was successful, both in gaining publicity and in boosting the morale of the group; on 16 May the squatters, hearing that the council was going to demolish these houses to make way for a car park, again occupied them and prevented the council workmen who arrived from commencing the demolition. This demonstration went so smoothly that the squatters ended up playing football with the demolition men. As before, the squat attracted widespread publicity in the town.

The Brighton Council meeting of 22 May was the scene of the next big housing rumpus. Members of the Rents Project picketed the Town Hall all day and when the council meeting started they filled the public gallery. It was as the council were discussing the housing issue that Mr Chris Baxter, a university lecturer, rose in the gallery and asked to be allowed to speak and present the petition with 2,000 signatures expressing 'public worry and concern about housing problems'. The 'representatives of the people' however were not interested: the Mayor adjourned the meeting and ordered the police to clear the gallery. This high-handed action led to scuffles and eleven people were arrested. The members of the Rents Project – students and tenants among them – now decided that more direct action was necessary and on 23 May the *Brighton and*

Hove Gazette carried the following statement from a Rents Project committee member: 'The idea is to place two families into empty houses and for the "squatters" to go in, defend and look after them.'

On 14 June the Brighton Squatters and the Rents Project carried out the first real squat in the town for twenty-three years when two families were moved into two empty council-owned houses in Terminus Road. The council had planned to leave the houses empty for years pending a redevelopment scheme and reacted quickly – but legally – by serving notice of an application for possession on the two families. These were heard in Brighton County Court on 2 July 1969 and resulted in the families being given twenty-eight days to quit and in being ordered to pay £7 damages to the council for trespass, despite the fact that they had in fact improved the houses. The council was obviously embarrassed by the publicity and made statements about using the houses for welfare purposes – and indeed later did this. The court proceedings, however, certainly did not have the effect the council desired and more families started squatting in empty council property in Terminus Road and nearby Railway Street. By the second week in July six families were squatting and moreover the two families under notice to quit had declared their intention of 'squatting for ten years if necessary'.

The council said publicly that they were prepared to 'discuss' the situation, but not under duress – that is, while squatting continued. The Brighton Rents Project and the squatters decided to test them. They had found a really excellent site on which to squat all six families and it was decided to move them out of the council property and into Wykeham Terrace, an empty row of army houses that had once been used as married quarters. The whole block was now due to be auctioned for private development. Saturday 19 July was earmarked for the move-in.

The occupation was brilliantly planned and went off without hitch. One house was opened and in swarmed the squatters, minutes later the first van full of furniture drew up and was hurriedly emptied. More houses were opened up and more furniture arrived on the scene. By the time the police, press, radio and the estate agent arrived the operation was complete.

This success had a deep effect on the families and their supporters: morale rose and a real spirit of solidarity and community feeling grew up amongst the families. A few days later, on 23 July, the property was due to be auctioned. As the owner could not at that time promise vacant possession the auction proved abortive, but it gave the squatters a good opportunity to make publicity. Bidders and observers were showered with leaflets declaring 'Wykeham Terrace belongs to the people not the profiteers,' and one attempt at land speculation was thus halted.

On 3 August the squatters extended their territory and occupied another huge complex of buildings at the rear of Wykeham Terrace, in Queens Square, with the intention of squatting four more families and using a large drill hall as a playground for the children. This new move was carried off as smoothly and efficiently as the initial occupation of Wykeham Terrace. Soon more families did move in until there were twelve altogether. The new 'acquisition' in Queens Square brought the squatters into renewed conflict with the council, who owned the houses although they were all part of the same block as Wykeham Terrace.

The owners of the other houses in Wykeham Terrace (the Territorial Army) and Queens Square (Brighton Council) spent a considerable length of time deciding what to do about the squatters. One thing was plain, however – they were not going to make the same mistake as Redbridge Council and act illegally. It was not until the end of September that they finally started to take anti-squatter measures. Long before that, however, things had started to go seriously wrong with the squat. If we in Ilford and those in Fulham had had trouble with certain elements as I have indicated, the idiotic and absolutely irresponsible behaviour of one or two people in Brighton was, if anything, worse. Bombs were made on the squat and used to blow up the local Army Information Office. Many of the more sensible members of the group were enraged by this act – their only mistake lay in allowing the situation to get as bad as it did.

However all the anger in the world could not retrieve the

situation that developed when some 'squatters' were arrested on an explosives charge following the explosion. It was this that brought the police into Wykeham Terrace with search warrants. It was this, too, that started the demoralization of some of the families. The net result of all this was the development of a rift between the squatters and the Rents Project, and the sensible members of the squatters – Andy Wright, Mick Mountford and 'Dave' to name only three who kept things going – found themselves with their backs to the wall – just at the time when maximum unity was needed.

In the middle of September Brighton Council was thus in a strong position, through no effort of its own, to launch a counter-offensive. On 26 September the drill hall, which had been used for storage by the squatters, was 'squatted' by the men in blue (even more ironic this, than the Redbridge Town Clerk's advocacy of direct action) until the council workmen arrived to board it up. The council then commenced High Court proceedings to have the families removed from Queens Square; these proved unnecessary when all the families in that block moved into Wykeham Terrace. It was thus up to the Territorial Army to get out all ten families that were still squatting and in October 1969 they began their attempts.

It is worthwhile discussing in some detail the method adopted by the Territorials as it was different from any other method so far mentioned. They applied for an *ex parte* blanket possession order against unnamed persons. In simple terms this means that they made an application for possession at which only they were represented (that is what *ex parte* means) and which would not be directed against a named person or people, but against everybody in the building. It gave the occupants no right to a hearing and also made the business of swapping families useless – as any order would be directed against everybody in the building. At Wykeham Terrace there was no evidence of forcible entry and although there probably was evidence of forcible detainer the Territorial Army sought to obtain a blanket possession order against people (as it must be) but *ex parte*, and against people unnamed, who thus had no right to put a defence. To the squatters movement this could have proved to be a very different obstacle.

Redbridge Council had not tried this means of removing us from their property because at the time *ex parte* blanket orders did not exist in law (and do not now). They had been introduced by, and allowed by, the vacation courts in September and October 1969 when the London Street Commune ('the hippies') had started occupying buildings in central London. They were unprecedented and a complete diversion from legal procedure.

In October, however, when the Territorial Army tried to use these precedents and obtain such an order against the families in Wykeham Terrace they got a nasty shock. By this time the anti-'hippy' hysteria had subsided and anyway families are quite different from 'hippies'. So it was that when the army tried to obtain an order *ex parte* a barrister, Mr Michael Walker, turned up at court representing Mrs Maureen Hales, one of the squatting mothers. Mr Justice Stamp, to his credit, did not immediately follow the precedent set in the 'hippy' case and adjourned the case to hear full legal arguments on the matter.

After a number of adjournments during which leading counsel was instructed to advise him (in addition to counsel for the Territorial Army and counsel for Mrs Hales), he decided on 13 November 1969 that *ex parte* possession orders were bad in law. How can any hearing pretend to take place in the High Court of *Justice* if the defendant is not allowed to present his defence? Mr Justice Stamp decided that he could not allow breaches of legal procedure just for the sake of convenience. His other objection to *ex parte* orders against unnamed persons was that by their very nature they were not directed at anybody specific. One cannot have a court order which does not order anybody.

Mr Justice Stamp's judgment was strengthened in a hearing in the Appeal Court on 14 January 1970, when Lord Diplock, in relation to a matter concerning the Manchester gypsies, also refused to grant an *ex parte* possession order. A decision in the Appeal Court thus effectively disposed of *ex parte* possession orders. Mr Justice Stamp did, however, grant a possession order against Mrs Hales as was expected and also gave the Territorial Army some advice on how to obtain possession of their property legally. Briefly his judgment was that the rest of the squatters in possession of Wykeham Terrace had eight days to enter their names as defendants in the action and so have a right to a defence. He also ruled that to nail a copy of his judgment on the outer door of every house was a valid service – thus preventing 'evasion of service' tactics being adopted. Failure of anyone to obey these instructions and enter a defence would result in a writ of possession being issued. However, delaying and avoiding tactics could now be adopted by the squatters – by entering the names of defendants, then swapping. The timing of the swaps and the method of proving them to the court would have to be carefully worked out – but it certainly seems possible to frustrate this method of obtaining possession by owners in the future.

It is always easy to be wise in retrospect, and the fact that rather complicated tactics were not adopted in Brighton is hardly a thing for which the Brighton group should be criticized. The most important fact was that, despite the difficulties and setbacks I have described, some squatters and members of the Rents Project continued to attempt to retrieve something from the situation. It is pure conjecture, of course, even to think what might have been the result in Brighton had not the catastrophic events of the summer months occurred.

On 23 November the families appealed to the (Labour) Prime Minister, who showed his concern by ignoring them. On 25 November the writ for possession was issued and on 28 November the Sheriff of Sussex executed the writ and evicted all nine families. The Brighton Welfare Department then had a statutory obligation to provide shelter for the families. Six of them were placed in empty sub-standard properties. Three families were not given accommodation of any kind – despite the National Assistance Act and government circulars on how to implement it. The excuse was that two of the families came from Hove and that the other one, although a Brighton family, had 'only one child (so) the committee felt that they should be able to find accommodation for themselves' (Mr R. N. Nicol, director of Brighton welfare services: the *Guardian*, 2 December 1969). So much for the law. Even an offer by Shelter to rehouse these three families within three months failed to alter the 'welfare' committee's decision. The families were forced to accept an offer of accommodation from Sussex University Students Union until they were offered accommodation by a well-wisher about three weeks later. The squat in Brighton was over.

For six families at least, squatting had not been a complete failure; for their squatting had achieved nothing. On the wider issues some small successes were achieved: the council certainly admitted to owning empty property and made certain noises about using it for welfare purposes in future. For some of the squatters' supporters, however, recent events have not been happy. Following the 'hippy' squats, the authorities successfully charged some members of the London Street Commune with conspiracy to commit forcible detainer at the Endell Street school. They were found guilty as they held the place 'with strong hand and multitude of people'. A way of using the Forcible Entry Act *against* squatters is a thing which the authorities had no doubt been looking into for some time. Five members of the Brighton squat were charged with the forcible detainer of Wykeham Terrace, contrary to the 1429 Forcible Entry Act. Some were eventually found guilty and sentenced to long terms of imprisonment. Therefore it is both relevant and important to consider why the Brighton Squatters were charged when we in Ilford were not. We were not guilty of forcible detainer when we stocked weapons to resist the eviction attempts of 25 June because we only stocked weapons *after* illegal forcible entries had taken place and when there was every reason to fear further illegal acts being committed against us. Thus we were only exercising our right to defend a dwelling house with force against an illegal entrant. The Brighton Squatters, on the other hand, fortified Wykeham Terrace both without the threat of illegal evictions taking place and against a legal eviction. A technicality this may be, but if squatters are going to frustrate the law by treading a path through its technicalities, they must tread very carefully indeed.

8. The Struggle Continues: South-East London

It is probably clear by now that the long struggle in Redbridge was the most vital one for the squatters campaign. Had we been crushed without much trouble there, not only would the squatters movement have suffered, but so too would the whole direct action housing movement. The authorities would have reversed the series of successes that had been achieved at the hostels and wrested the initiative from us. No longer would they have feared a militant campaign. The fact that we were successful means that the movement spread, usually winning considerable concessions. It was in south-east London however that the new situation was exploited to the full – and is still being exploited. There the wariness of the authorities after Redbridge was used to build up a highly successful squatters group; there the authorities were forced to give in every time. If we in east London had developed our legal manoeuvres to the highest possible degree, it was in south-east London that the tactic of 'ultra-reasonableness' was most highly developed.

That an active group should develop in south-east London was almost inevitable with Jim Radford and other militants from the King Hill struggle living there. At first glance what is surprising is that it took the group so long to organize its first squat. On closer examination, however, we can understand why. A number of the activists from south-east London became involved in the squatters movement very early in 1969 and Jim Radford had, of course, been involved from the very beginning. A South-East London Squatters group was formed in January 1969 mainly centred around a homeless hostel run by the London Borough of Greenwich called Plumstead Lodge.

In April 1969, after a couple of token squats, they installed their first family in the London Borough of Bromley.

It was in Lewisham, however, that the South-East London

Squatters' tactic of 'ultra-reasonableness' really made progress. Herbert Eames, the borough's housing chairman, is an intelligent and reasonable man. The squatters took up their first case, that of Heather Bonadie, a divorcee who lived in such appalling conditions that she lost the custody of two of her three children. She suffered from acute thyroid herself and was told by her doctor that she must leave her flat. After Lewisham Council refused to rehouse her, the squatters moved her into an empty house owned by the council which was not due for redevelopment for nearly a year. The South-East London Squatters publicized the background to the squat and asked what possible objection there could be to Heather being allowed to remain in the house until the council wished to demolish it for redevelopment. Faced with this and bearing in mind what was happening in Redbridge, Lewisham Borough Council was in a very unenviable position.

On 10 June it was announced that Heather Bonadie was to be allowed to stay in the house. Councillor Eames said 'she can stay there until the place is pulled down' (*Guardian*, 11 June 1969). Another spokesman for Lewisham Council announced: 'We have taken the word of the squatters association that this family will be moved out when the time comes' (*Lewisham Journal*, 12 June 1969). When Lewisham Council first met to discuss the plan, on 17 June, they threw it out, but four days later reversed the decision and agreed to allow *bona fide* organizations to occupy the empty houses in the borough. A vociferous minority that had been opposed to the idea was defeated. On 25 June, the day of the battles in Ilford, Lewisham Council ratified the proposal.

It may surprise some people to discover that Herbert Eames is also a Tory, and that the London Borough of Lewisham had at that time a Tory council. It is also worth noting that Lewisham Welfare Department has no hostels. Homeless people in the borough are put into short-life property, usually after a brief stay in a reception unit.[1]

1. I must point out, however, that I have had many clashes with the officers in the homeless families section who turned away homeless families seeking accommodation. Lewisham, like all other boroughs, simply does not, unless pushed, accept all homeless families into its temporary accommodation.

However, despite the council's decision to allow *bona fide* organizations to use their empty houses, nothing had happened. For none of these organizations showed much interest. It was left to the South-East London Squatters to take the council at their word and to get things organized in the borough. One problem in particular had to be resolved before any project could get under way; it concerned the way in which squatting in short-life property would affect a family's housing points. This is of immense importance to the whole project and the arrangement finally worked out in Lewisham could be, and has been, used as a blueprint for similar arrangements elsewhere.

Families on council housing lists receive points and the more points a family has the nearer they come to being rehoused. Points are awarded for numerous reasons, among the most important being the condition of the existing accommodation, the degree of overcrowding and the facilities enjoyed by the family (e.g. whether they have to share a toilet, etc.). The squatters' intention in Lewisham was to install families living in very bad conditions in short-life property which, although not perfect, would be far superior to the accommodation from which they came. Clearly, if the normal council practice was adopted, squatting families would lose points, as they would move into better conditions. This in turn would have the effect of pushing the family down the housing queue and possibly even of making them perpetual squatters as their squatting conditions could put them too low on the list for permanent rehousing. This was obviously unsatisfactory and would make the scheme unworkable. The aim of the squatters was that families should live in reasonable conditions prior to permanent rehousing and certainly not to push the families down the housing list and thus relieve the council of any responsibility for the families. This is a basic difference between the Lewisham squatters and a housing association.

An arrangement was reached between the squatting association and the council that families who squatted in short-life property would not lose points – they would continue to be assessed on the basis of their old conditions. The only difference that squatting would make was that when their case came before the housing committee for consideration (on the basis of their old points) the committee would take into account the fact that the family was squatting and might defer the case – but only until the end of the life of the house they were squatting in; at that point, if the family had, on the basis of its pre-squatting points, reached the top of the housing list when their house was demolished, the council would rehouse them. There would be, thus, no chance of families becoming permanent squatters or being pushed further down the housing list. The families would gain much and lose little, while the squatting association would have achieved its primary aim of both helping families and not allowing the council to avoid its responsibilities. In return for this agreement the association guaranteed two things only. First, to move only Lewisham families into the houses and, second, to give the council vacant possession of the premises as soon as they were needed for redevelopment.

This agreement was not reached until the first week of December, but by the middle of November it was sufficiently clear that a satisfactory arrangement was pending for the Lewisham project to start being organized. On 15 October a meeting was organized in Catford Town Hall by the South-East London Squatters. A wide variety of people from all the political parties and from numerous other organizations in Lewisham attended, and the Lewisham Family Squatting Association was born. The aims of the LFSA are easily stated. They are to squat Lewisham families in accordance with the agreement I have just outlined in short-life property belonging to the council. The association would work at all times in full co-operation with the council. For their part the council drew up a list of eighty-eight empty properties that could be used. Mr Rowe, the council's lettings officer, makes the decision easier for those families intending to squat by informing them approximately when the council feel that the family will be offered permanent accommodation. This is a great advantage as, clearly, if a family has a good chance of being rehoused within, say, a few weeks then it would probably not be in their interest to squat.

The council also agreed to an arrangement concerning families that have not even qualified for consideration for a house. All London boroughs have a one-year waiting period which families must go through before they are visited by the housing department, assessed, and have their case considered. Families must also have been resident somewhere in the London area for five years before they are assessed and considered. Many of the families who have approached us in Lewisham do not satisfy either the one-year borough waiting qualification or the five-year London residential qualification. In the past, if a family decided to squat then, by the time they had qualified for assessment, they would have been out of their bad old conditions for some time and would be living in a squatting house. The Lewisham housing department therefore arranges immediate visits for these families so that when they do qualify they are assessed on their old pointage. Those families who have had to hand back their houses before they reach the top of the housing list will either be re-squatted in another empty house by the LFSA or they will be adopted and rehoused by the Quadrant Housing Society.

Contrary to what many people believe, the aim of the squatters movement from its inception was to occupy houses and offer to pay rent for them. Indeed the demand for a rent book was at the forefront of all squats; the Lewisham group was no exception. In fact, when Heather Bonadie started to squat, she wrote to the council offering to pay rent and rates and also to vacate the property when it was required for redevelopment. As soon as the LFSA started operations – indeed even before – badly housed families started to inquire about squatting. It was explained to them just what squatting in Lewisham was all about; that there were no landlords and no tenants, but instead they would all be members; that most of the work would have to be done by them; that the taking of decisions rested with them; in short that control was in their hands and the future of the group was dependent on them. All families had to attend meetings before becoming members of the group. This membership of course would then entitle families to be helped by the group to occupy empty houses. The houses were made ready by work parties of families who turned out on Saturdays or in the evenings. The group was thus able to get houses

repaired very cheaply and quickly, and many apparently unusable houses were brought back into use.

Policy decisions had to be made by the general meeting to
which all families were encouraged to come. I had been
appointed full-time co-ordinator and had to explain and often
justify all the 'administrative' decisions that I had taken week
by week. As more and more families took up occupation of the
houses, so the general meetings got larger and larger. During
the summer and autumn of 1970 the average weekly attendance was over 100 people – all but a few of them being squatting families. It was these meetings that took all the decisions
or approved or rejected all committee recommendations. They
became a weekly outing for everybody as well as a squatters
meeting: morale was high and attendance good. Slanging
matches, abuse, verbal battles and policy rows were common,
but throughout it all a real sense of comradeship developed
among the families who had previously, largely because of their
appalling housing conditions, been depressed, apathetic and
downcast. One of the best features of the group was that black
and white people would work together, row together, drink together. The arguments would result in people taking sides – but
not on colour grounds. As one squatter, Charlie Hazel, once
said after seeing a television programme about racial integra-
tion: 'They should come down and film the Lewisham Squatters. We're a good example of black and white working together.'

On the other side, it must be admitted that there were problems. There were families that did not play their part in the
group, merely took their houses and let the other families help
them, but did nothing in return. There were also some that did
not pay their weekly 'rents'. The problems created by these
caused row after row at general meetings. Committee members
were delegated to visit them, neighbouring families visited
them, they were asked to attend general meetings. After repeated requests they were told that their 'miscreance' would be
discussed openly at general meetings if they did not present
some kind of general explanation. All this worked to some
extent but not completely.

The issue came to a head in February 1971, when a large

number of families revolted in a protest against the association's lack of action against these families. The one area in which the non-squatting families had exercised most influence had been here, and we had stood out against any move to evict the unco-operative families. But the majority would stand for this no longer and they were determined to face the problem. They elected their (virtually) all-family committee which decided that one or two of the really worst families should be told in no uncertain terms to pull their weight or get out. It was not simply a question of 'rent' arrears – the whole lack of participation by these families was also involved and in one case a woman had successfully terrorized other squatting families. A lengthy process was then adopted: the families concerned would be summoned to appear before the committee and if they presented any explanation and started to pull their weight in the future then no action would be taken. If there was neither explanation nor change then the committee would recommend to the general meeting that the association should take action to evict the family concerned. The general meeting would have to ratify this and the family could, of course, attend and argue their case. Even after the general meeting had ratified the action, the committee or the staff were given power to suspend it if there was any change. This lengthy procedure gave considerable time for families to alter their ways, and considerable opportunity to put their case. The result was that, although the initial decision to evict was taken in February, it was not until October and November that the two very worst families were actually evicted by the association.

One of the complaints raised against the LFSA is that they have 'sold out' and become 'good boys' in the pockets of the council. In the early days this accusation was made against us by a group of communards who threatened to wreck the whole project. They refused to move from a house reclaimed for redevelopment by the council. We spent hour after hour, night after night, explaining to the occupants that if we failed to hand back the house we stood to lose 100 houses for families with children, and that the whole system would be wrecked. The 'communards' were unmoved. Only after hours and nights spent at the 'commune' by Jim Radford and many offers of help, was the resistance finally talked out of the 'communards' and they agreed to leave the house on 10 January with our help in moving them. The 'communards', who had no previous involvement in the campaign, accused us of 'selling out', although it was never explained how getting families homes and giving them control of them, was selling out the aims of the movement. It seems to me that the most revolutionary thing in the world is to demonstrate to the disfranchized, alienated and therefore apathetic majority of people that they *can* act and win, and that they *can* run their own lives without rulers, politicians and their ilk.

On numerous occasions the LFSA had been compelled to take direct action at the homeless families department of Lewisham Council as, despite the council's duty and its claim that all homeless families receive temporary accommodation, we had often been faced with families who were literally homeless, being refused accommodation by the department. On other occasions we would urge the public health department to act, or ensure that the housing department had families correctly pointed. We would put pressure on the GLC to rehouse families; we would stop illegal evictions by landlords, and push the council to prosecute them. In short, many awkward and unusual cases were brought to the LSFA office and we would take them up, our action sometimes being backed up by Lewisham squatting families arriving to give physical support.

The group continued to grow democratically: in September at the AGM a number of new families were elected to the LFSA committee, and in January 1971 Bob Clayton, former co-ordinator of the Southwark squatters, took over my job as LFSA field officer. We were able to demonstrate that there was no difficulty in keeping our side of the agreement, by successfully moving thirty-seven families out of Adolphus Street in Deptford when the site was needed for redevelopment. Many of these families now qualified for council housing, the remainder were either re-squatted or housed by the Quadrant Housing Association. This success was of great value in future bargaining with the council.

One major problem facing the LFSA concerned the coming to power in Lewisham of the Labour Party after the May election. We knew that many Labour councillors were still very antagonistic towards the squatters. The 'vociferous minority' on Lewisham Council who had strongly opposed the council's conciliatory attitude were the Labour minority. Councillor Albert Scutt, General Secretary and Agent of Deptford Labour Party, put their position very clearly in a letter to the *South East London Mercury* on 10 July, when he wrote:

The Labour members on the committee, with the support of several Tory members, were determined to resist the unlawful acts of the squatters, who are undoubtedly pursuing the law of the jungle.

Councillor Scutt, who had denounced the Tories for allowing the LFSA arrangement in the first place, was completely unrepentant. A confidential internal document of the Labour group that we had got hold of said that it was their policy to 'take over' the squatters and 'phase out' the LFSA. While we could have no objection to the council making greater use of short-life houses themselves – particularly after our hammering at the homeless families department to get more accommodation for the families they frequently turned away – we certainly did not want to surrender our independence. In addition we were somewhat sceptical of the council's ability to organize the LFSA and of their ability to use many of the houses we had repaired. There were a number of informal discussions with the new Labour chairman, Councillor Fred Winslade, and the new leader of the council, Councillor Andy Hawkins. There was also a formal meeting with them both and with Councillor Ron Pepper. Councillor Hawkins was friendly and Councillor Winslade seemed to be won round, but Councillor Pepper remained antagonistic to squatting. The final result was that, although the council started to use more short-life property than it had been using, it decided not to try to take over the LFSA.

With the policy of co-operation the squatters housed many families. The council had started by giving the association the list of eighty-eight empty properties. Fifteen of these were considered acceptable and five families were found who wanted to squat. As news of the squatters spread, more and more families approached the LFSA. Some heard about the squatters through personal contacts, or friends, or the newspapers, others were referred to us by social workers, teachers, psychiatrists, probation officers, health visitors, the Citizens Advice Bureau, or indeed just about anybody. In the first year of its existence the association housed some 100 families in houses handed over to it both by the Lewisham Borough Council and by the GLC. However, it soon became clear that there would be more families than houses and this meant that a system of selection had to be adopted. There seems to be no other way of allocating houses. Of course the group pushed for more houses and often obtained them – but the problem remained. However, despite all this and despite its growing local success, the South-East London Squatters kept up their interest in other boroughs. They pushed Greenwich, Southwark and even Brent councils to take in families. Bromley council was the main target: their Welfare Department is particularly renowned for turning away homeless families. One – the Gowers – were eventually squatted in Annerley by a task force of Lewisham families. They were finally rehoused by Bromley Council.

Maximum co-operation and self-government among the squatting families was always our policy. However, it was necessary to have a separate committee as it is impossible to discuss fifty applications to squat in a meeting of a hundred people. It is undesirable to discuss 'rent arrears' in open meetings, and this was only done, as I have said, after great efforts to find some reasons for these had failed. These matters were therefore discussed by the committee, but the policy which they would implement was always laid down by general meetings. Thus it was the general meeting that authorized the committee what factors to consider when families applied to squat; it was the general meeting that laid down the procedure for dealing with rent arrears; it was the general meeting that I had to report to.

The committee initially consisted of non-families, simply because it was non-squatting people who had got things going. Clearly families could not be elected to the committee until they had approached the LFSA. During the early months of

1970 a number of families were elected to the committee on various occasions, but only occasionally did they play a major role. I must admit that this was a great mistake on the part of the non-families and it caused an 'us' and 'them' feeling to develop to some extent.

Had any families come forward to take control they would not have met with any opposition – indeed Jim Radford repeatedly urged this. In February 1971 however the squatting families did take over the committee because the non-squatters refused to be on it any longer. Since then they have been very much in control of things, and there is no doubt that the Lewisham Family Squatting Association, which is still going strong, and has now housed some 200 families, has shown that ordinary working people *are* capable of effectively taking action to help themselves, and *can* organize their own lives.

9. Arbour Square

During Redbridge we had formed a 'front group' called the Campaign to Clear Hostels and Slums, the purpose of which was to retain a certain degree of 'respectability' (and even try to register as a charity) and so raise money for the squatters.[1] Tony Mahony became its full-time organizer and an office was rented in Osborne Street E1. The CCHS was not successful at money-raising, but it did develop a number of contacts with homeless and badly housed families around Stepney and was involved in the formation of tenants associations in tenement blocks. Three families living in dreadful conditions in Cheshire Street E1, heard about CCHS and contacted Tony. Two of these families were keen to squat, so Tony looked around for a suitable place, with the result that on Saturday 27 September 1969 Stepney police station received some new neighbours when three families (two from Cheshire Street) occupied three flats in a large, nearly empty block next door to the police station in Arbour Square E1. Of the seventy or so flats in the block some sixty were empty and many of them had been so for nearly two years. That empty flats should exist in Stepney of all places is perhaps the biggest imaginable insult to London's slum dwellers. Tower Hamlets Council, who owned them, claimed that they were being cleared for modernization. Even on the surface this seemed pretty thin, as two years was a long time for the flats to be empty. On a closer examination however the reasons offered by Tower Hamlets Council were even less credible.

About five minutes' walk from Arbour Square is Beechcroft

1. Ironically, some of the people most opposed to the Family Squatting Advisory Service which obtains money from Shelter (see Chapter 10) were involved in CCHS, despite the fact that the role CCHS was to play would have been similar to that which the FSAS now does.

Buildings, which is the Tower Hamlets Welfare Department Part III Accommodation. Compared with this place Arbour Square, which admittedly did need modernizing, was a palace. Why should the council choose one of the best blocks in the area to modernize when Beechcroft Buildings was far more in need of improvement? Where the council's case really fell down, however, was over the length of time the flats had been empty. The council wanted all seventy flats empty before it started modernization, but this would seem to be unnecessary. There was no apparent reason why work could not be commenced as rows, of say six, became vacant. In September 1969 sixty out of seventy were empty, including whole floors. The work on many of them could easily have been started and, indeed, finished on some blocks, which could then have been reoccupied. The Arbour Square block appeared therefore to be an example of bureaucratic incompetence at its worst. Finally, if the council did need all the flats empty before they could start on the modernization, then Arbour Square was just like any other clearance area and various squatting associations have shown how short-life properties can be used.

On 27 September only three families had squatted in Arbour Square, but within a few days there were six. One of the original three, incidentally, was the McNallys who had successfully squatted for so long in Ilford with the permission of the owner of the house. Having got all their children out of care the McNallys were keen to return to Tower Hamlets, where they originally came from. Tony Mahony approached Jack Wolkind, the Town Clerk of Tower Hamlets, and offered to discuss things. Mr Wolkind argued that the council was in a difficult position with all the east London slums within its boundaries. Tony explained that he understood this, and to avoid a confrontation he suggested a settlement so that the CCHS and the all-Labour–Communist council could work jointly in an effort to fight the housing conditions in east London. Jack Wolkind is a sensible man and he seemed interested, but he is not the leader of the council. Alderman Orwell is the leader and policy is made by him and other committee chairmen. These men decided to fight and tried to use the courts to beat the squatters. They obtained High Court interim injunctions restraining the families from continuing their trespass on Arbour Square pending the hearing of an application for possession. These injunctions were also directed against a local journalist, Tony Mahony and me – and I had never been near the place. One would have thought that at least the council would have learnt from Redbridge's mistakes.

In October 1969 there were two preliminary court hearings, which resulted simply in the injunctions being continued. The squatting families and Tony, however, ignored them. The council was faced with the choice either of allowing this to continue or of having them all committed to prison for contempt of court. Apart from any public outcry there were the children to consider. Had the parents been imprisoned they would have to be taken into care – and this would have cost the council about £15 per week per child. Thus Tower Hamlets Council had obtained their legal 'big stick' but could not wield it. So far as the actual hearing of the application for possession orders in the courts was concerned there was a very considerable delay before the hearings were actually set down. In fact through the end of 1969 and the early months of 1970 there were numerous adjournments. The squatters had discovered that the council might have failed to act in accordance with its own standing orders in initiating legal proceedings, as the action had been commenced before a meeting of the council's General Purposes Committee had authorized it. The squatters also took legal advice as to whether they could fight the case and were informed that there might be a possibility of arguing that 'necessity' had forced the families to squat and commit what would otherwise be unlawful acts: therefore, it could be argued, the possession order ought not to be granted. The squatters applied for legal aid to argue this case, and when this was refused, they appealed, but unsuccessfully. This led to further delay and the case was not finally heard until the summer of 1970.

Meanwhile more families had squatted in Arbour Square and, although some had left, the number had reached twenty. Tony Mahony was still working with the squat, and a squat 'office' grew up at the house of Clive Dixon in Aylward Street, just round the corner from Arbour House. There were a number of demonstrations by the squatters and some noisy scenes in the council chamber. One demonstration was of particular importance, and it occurred when the London Electricity Board, on the instructions of the council, dug up and disconnected the services from the whole of Arbour House. This action by the LEB is of dubious legality and anyway it certainly annoyed and alarmed the squatters. It meant that the families had no light and no cooking facilities as they were using electric cookers; this could have made things very difficult for them. Until this point I had not been involved in the campaign at all; indeed I had only twice visited Arbour House and the first I heard of these events was when I received a telephone call in the Lewisham office from one of the squatters. My advice was to try to obtain an injunction requiring the LEB to fulfill their responsibility and to supply electricity under the Electricity Supply Acts. However, on further discussion it became clear that this was impractical and I then advised the squatters to go *en masse* to the council's Welfare Department and symbolically 'dump' all their children on the council as it was not possible to live without light or cooking facilities. This worked: the next day the LEB, again acting on council instructions, reconnected the services and the squat continued. This was my only intervention in the Arbour Square squat until September 1970.

Eventually the cases came to court and were heard in August 1970. The campaign had by this time become somewhat disorganized and the plan, to argue the case on the grounds of necessity and the council's breach of standing orders, came to nothing. In addition, the continued political squabbles among most of the helpers of the squat had caused morale among the families to sink to rock bottom, with the result that unity declined and inter-family feuds developed. Bitterness grew up at a time when greatest solidarity was needed. Despite the efforts of Tony Mahony, who persistently tried to keep the campaign going, when the cases got to court the squatters were in no state to put up much resistance. The first possession orders were granted and they expired at the beginning of September. At this point the squatters appealed to the council for negotiations, and finally, nearly a year after the squat had begun, Tony Mahony and five squatting families met the leader of the council, Councillor William Guy, deputy leader Alderman Tom Mitchell and council officers at Bethnal Green Town Hall on 14 September. It is worth noting that, during the entire duration of the squat, communist Councillors Barney Bormann and Solly Kaye did nothing to help the squatters. An appeal to TUC Secretary Mr Feather also proved fruitless. The squatters therefore had drawn up a document for the meeting, entitled 'Alternatives to Eviction', which suggested ways in which a peaceful solution might be arrived at.

Tony Mahony and the families were well aware that they would have to make sensible demands on the council and, as the more 'hard line' of the helpers left the squat, a reasoned document was drawn up. The talks however lasted only twenty minutes, after which the squatters walked out. The meeting had not been friendly and talks didn't get off the ground: the stumbling block was the squatters' demand that any action on the court orders be suspended, and Councillor Guy's reply that he could not give such an undertaking, but could only take the matter to the whole council.

The campaign was in disarray: the families were bitter and demoralized. The self-styled militants who had steered a confrontationist course for the squat and denounced all negotiations as 'reformist sell-outs' *had disappeared from the scene*. The families, at the very time they needed help most, were abandoned by all their 'militant supporters' with the exception of Tony Mahony and Clive Dixon.

It was at that time that I decided to intervene in Arbour Square in order to try to set up a Lewisham-style group. I decided that the best approach would be direct to the council leader William Guy, and on 15 September 1970 I telephoned him. I judged that the possession orders that had been granted, and the ones soon to follow, would put great pressure on the council – the possibility of having to provide temporary accommodation for some twenty-five families would be quite a headache for them. Alternatively they could refuse to provide temporary accommodation but, as this might mean many children being taken into care, this also would present them with

quite a problem. In the event I later discovered that the council
had decided to offer temporary accommodation to all 'Tower
Hamlets families' – that is families who had been resident in
the borough before squatting in Arbour House; no accommodation was to be offered to families who had come from
outside the borough, while arrangements had been made with
other London boroughs to offer temporary accommodation to
families who had been resident in their boundaries before coming to Arbour House. This arrangement clearly lessened the
problem for the council, but still presented a difficult task, and
in addition twenty-five evictions would attract considerable
publicity.

It was with all this in mind that I phoned Councillor Guy
and suggested there might be a way of solving things. His
reaction was not friendly but finally, after I had wildly and in
desperation offered to clear Arbour House peacefully, he
agreed to let me discuss things with deputy Town Clerk Mr
Phillip Marrett. I met Mr Marrett on the same day at 3 p.m.
and put to him my proposals for setting up a Lewisham-type
squatting group. I said that this could result in the peaceful
clearing of Arbour House which would be to the benefit both of
the families who would be rehoused by the group, and of the
council which would be able to avoid a number of unpleasant
evictions. Mr Marrett seemed pleased at these proposals and
agreed to pass them on to the leader of the council and the
other council officers for consideration. I did not have to wait
long for an indication that the council was prepared to negotiate, for on returning to the Lewisham office I received a
telephone call from Mr Marrett informing me that he had
spoken to the leader of the council who was interested. This
was a tentative but important beginning and I now had the
unenviable task of approaching the Arbour Square squatters.
At about 1 a.m. on 16 September I therefore went to see Tony
Mahony and explained to him what I had done. Tony was
immensely relieved that there seemed a possibility of salvaging
something from the situation and later that day he passed the
information on to the squatting families. A demonstration had
been planned for the council meeting that very night, 16 September, but instead the squatters listened quietly while Council-

lor Guy read a carefully prepared statement that 'an organization' had put certain proposals to the council and that while these were being discussed, although the council would continue to obtain possession orders against the rest of the families, all action on them would be suspended. This meant there would be no evictions, and so the pressure on the squatters was lifted slightly.

Things were by no means settled, though, and I had as hard a job talking to the squatters as I had convincing the council of the idea. During October and November I had a number of meetings with the council's senior officers and finally the Housing (Letting and Management) Committee approved the scheme on 17 December, and their recommendations passed through the whole council on 27 January 1971.

It is, I think, fair to record therefore that without the help of a number of senior and chief officers of the council, it is unlikely that this scheme would have got through. So far as the Arbour Square squatters were concerned, I had to convince them that I was neither there to sell them out nor to evict them. The one thing that I stressed repeatedly was that I was not there to 'take over' and that if they accepted the deal I was negotiating, then I would not be running the new Tower Hamlets Family Squatting Association – they would. Eventually a committee was elected and following the council meeting of 27 January the first four houses were handed over to the THFSA. At this point, so keen was I, neither to take over nor lay myself open to charges of doing so, that I largely withdrew from the group. This however was a mistake and it nearly resulted in the association collapsing in chaos. There is clearly a difference in taking over and being around to give advice in the early stages. I thus went back into activity and slowly after this bad beginning the association became better organized. Unlike Lewisham in the early days, the Tower Hamlets Family Squatting Association committee always consisted of a majority of squatting families, and they were in no way reticent about putting their views. Slowly Arbour Square was cleared – our deadline was 1 August, as the council would have to renegotiate the contract if they could not give the contractors vacant possession by that date, and we rehoused the last family with one day to spare, on 31 July. The non-Tower Hamlets families had at first proved a problem as we had agreed only to rehouse them in houses obtained from the GLC and our initial efforts to obtain these were unsuccessful as those houses we had expected turned out to be unfit. Finally, however, we secured some GLC houses and were able to rehouse all the families. We had meanwhile successfully negotiated with Newham and Camden to continue to accept responsibility for Arbour Square families who came under their auspices, so that they would eventually be able to obtain council accommodation.

Since August the association has grown and there are now over sixty families in occupation. Thirstine Basset who had previously helped in Southwark and Lewisham was employed as co-ordinator in September, and various handymen have been paid to make repairs. As in Lewisham all decisions are made by the families – the amount of the 'rents', how they are spent, who gets the houses, what the association does. In fact the Tower Hamlets group has set a precedent by dispensing with a committee, at any rate for the time being, and all decisions are made at the weekly general meetings. One feature of the Tower Hamlets group that is rather different from all the others is the squatter-council agreement. In most boroughs this is quite short, but in Tower Hamlets the council has decided to affix its common seal to an exhaustive legal document. Negotiations have been going on about this for months and have only recently been completed. Council solicitor David Lewis has been most reasonable in amending many points at our request. The document, which provides for an informal working party to meet periodically to discuss progress, and sets up an arbitration procedure for disputes, in addition to laying down arrangements for the handing over and occupation of houses, has already been very useful in other areas and could prove a general model for future negotiations with many councils.

10. Southwark: A New Legal Situation

The Lewisham Family Squatting Association became an advice and action centre for the whole of south-east London. I have also refuted the criticism sometimes levelled at the group that it has sold its soul for a few houses and turned into a group of good boys. This criticism is refuted most clearly by the commencement in September 1970 of the long campaign in Southwark. In this borough the squatting movement fought its longest struggle against an authority bitterly opposed to it. In Southwark it faced the new legal techniques to remove squatters introduced by the High Court after the 'hippy' squats. It was in Southwark that we faced and confronted an enemy that did not make the major blunder, as had Redbridge, of acting illegally and violently and employing private armies of bailiffs.

The campaign began on 10 September 1970, but a number of important events had already taken place before that date. During 1970 the Lewisham group had been approached for help two or three times by individual families who had squatted on their own in Southwark. Jim Radford had therefore spoken to the council on their behalf and each time the Housing Department had adopted a conciliatory line and the families had been rehoused. Two points of importance must be clearly made here: first, that these squats were not inspired by Jim or myself or anyone else in Lewisham, and we had only subsequently been asked for help; second, that on all these occasions when Jim had spoken to the council he had suggested extending the Lewisham arrangement to Southwark, and had asked for discussions on this. All approaches had been ignored.

The squatters, however, were not the only people who had shown an interest in empty houses in Southwark prior to September 1970. At least two housing associations had approached the council with a view to being allowed to use some of the many vacant properties in the borough. From December 1969 to February 1970 Antony Fletcher of Quadrant had tried to obtain houses and, despite the fact that the then Town Clerk, Mr Dixon Ward, was favourable, the approach by Quadrant came to nothing. In July 1970 Southwark Council was again approached by a housing association – the Co-ownership Development Society – wishing to use short-life houses in the borough. CDS received a letter from Mr J. O'Brien, the Property Surveyor, to the effect that all short-life houses in the borough, even those with six months' life, were used by the council; thus another approach was rejected.

It was against this background that the squatters moved into Southwark. The actual 'move in' came when two homeless families in the borough were refused temporary accommodation by the homeless families department. George Anderson and his family were living in Lausanne Road SE 15, and were keen to move. Their landlord also wanted them out and began illegally harassing the family. He even changed the lock on the door. The harassment worked and the Andersons were homeless. They then contacted the Lewisham Family Squatting Association. I contacted the Southwark homeless families department on their behalf, but no offer of accommodation was forthcoming. At the same time Peter Williams and his family became homeless. Initially they had lived in Deal, Kent, and had been turned out when the house they had been living in changed hands. Unable to find any alternative accommodation in Kent they travelled to London to look for a home, and stayed for two weeks with friends in Swan Lane, Southwark. Eventually the friends, frightened themselves of getting into trouble with the council, their landlords, for having sub-tenants, had to ask the Williams to leave. This family also approached the homeless families department, and were also refused accommodation, being told to return to Deal. With nowhere to go in Deal the family could hardly do this, and so this irresponsible act of Southwark Council drove this family to approach the Lewisham squatters as well.

Thus in September 1970 we had two homeless families from Southwark virtually living in the Lewisham office. Southwark being adjacent to Lewisham, I had seen hundreds of empty houses. With two homeless families in my office it seemed reasonable to squat them in one of these. On 10 September therefore the Williams and Anderson families moved into 32 and 38 Harders Road, Peckham, SE 15. Both these houses were not due to be demolished until late 1972 and both were destined to remain empty until that time. They were also quite fit to live in – indeed they were officially classified as 'fit' properties – especially for families literally on the streets. Although Harders Road had been badly vandalized by the council – floorboards up, pipes ripped out, toilet cemented etc., a work party of Lewisham squatting families soon had it repaired. One Lewisham family even mended a hole in the wall. The Andersons and the Williams thus had homes. Two days later these two families were joined by Moses Adeyemo and his family, who moved from one tiny room to 15 Mortlock Gardens SE 15, just round the corner from the Anderson and Williams families. The Adeyemo's previous accommodation was so inadequate that they were separated from one of their children. Soon two more families joined the other three and by 24 September there were five squatting families in Southwark.

Meanwhile, immediately after the first squat, Jim Radford had sent to every Southwark councillor a detailed explanation of how the Lewisham scheme worked, an assurance that we were not looking for a confrontation and had only moved into Southwark because we had been forced to by the homeless families in our office, and a plea for Southwark Council to adopt a Lewisham-type scheme. He also asked them at least to discuss things, and meet us before they made up their minds. For two weeks we all waited, until on 24 September Jim and I were summoned to Peckham Town Hall, where we met council leader John O'Grady, chief executive Samuel Evans and assistant Town Clerk Thomas Thomas. We were told point blank that the council had rejected our request for a Lewisham scheme to operate in Southwark. We tried to elicit their reasons for this, and overcome their objections, but it was useless. The meeting between us and the council was not a discussion: it was designed to present us with a decision; indeed the council already had a press conference arranged for an hour later and a press statement prepared. Not only had the council turned down the squatters' proposal, they had even rejected the plea to discuss the matter with us before making up their minds.

An immediate call went out for help and that night we held a meeting attended by all the Southwark squatting families, a number of Lewisham families and numerous other supporters. The Southwark Family Squatting Association was formed to fight the evictions the council had threatened in their press statement and to try and persuade them to alter their policy. The tone of the council's statement suggested to us that this might be a long and tough struggle so we prepared ourselves accordingly. It was felt that, after the Redbridge experience and with Quartermain facing trial at the Old Bailey, the council would not use illegal methods. We decided therefore that we had to isolate them by a very reasoned argument and a generally over-conciliatory approach, as well as holding demonstrations to publicize the squat.

Further appeals were put to the council, and squatters frequently offered to vacate any houses that the council were going to use. The council had announced new plans to 'patch repair' and use some of the empty houses in redevelopment areas, and they claimed the squatters were holding this up by occupying some of the houses. 'Tell us which ones you want to use, and we'll voluntarily move out,' said the squatters. 'We only want houses that you are not going to use.' The Labour-controlled Southwark Council's only reply, however, was to issue originating summonses against all families squatting – there were nine by the beginning of October. 'Please,' begged the squatters, 'let's not have a confrontation. If you say you are interested in helping the badly housed of Southwark, so are we. Let's discuss our differences – we'll voluntarily move out of any houses we've occupied that you want to use if you'll just tell us which ones you intend not to use so we can repair them. We'll also sign legal undertakings to vacate when the time comes for demolition.' The council made no reply.

Following Mr Justice Stamp's ruling that *ex parte* possession orders were 'bad in law', one of the last acts of the Labour Government had been to authorize the new High Court Order

113 by which the authorities, learning from these cases, gave themselves a way quickly to evict squatters from property. It was Order 113 that Southwark Council now used against the Southwark squatters, and it is clear from the statements of Southwark Council at this time that they had considered this order in some detail, and seriously thought that it was a quick way in which to get us out of the borough.

The order meant that the plaintiff (the council) had simply to file various documents and papers on the squatters. A preliminary hearing before a High Court Master would see that this was done properly and then a date could be set, about a week later, for the full hearing before the Vice-Chancellor. The normal long wait before a hearing was thus avoided. In addition, the order also gave the judge power to make an immediate possession order, but worse still for the defendants (the squatters), the plaintiffs simply obtained their order as of right, after submitting affidavit evidence.[1] Thus the case could be heard extremely quickly, the hearing would be short, the order could be immediate and it was up to us to show that we had a legal defence which warranted a full trial which would be heard months later. The council, being the legal owner of the houses, was of the opinion that we could not do this. On 10 October the first preliminary court hearings before a High Court Master were heard and the 21st was set for the proper hearing before the Vice-Chancellor, Mr Justice Pennycuick, in the Chancery Division of the High Court.

The council looked forward to speedily crushing all opposition. It was therefore of the first importance that we find a way of avoiding Order 113 either by defeating it completely, or by delaying its workings. We had looked into the matter in some detail and we set about doing just that. Our defence was 'necessity'. The squatters, we argued, were driven to squat by sheer necessity, often worsened or even created by the council's failure to provide temporary accommodation for the families under Part III S21 of the 1948 National Assistance Act. On 19 October we thus filed some twenty-five affidavits containing evidence from clergymen, social workers, teachers,

1. i.e., sworn statements by witnesses obviating the need for them to appear in person.

psychiatrists, psychiatric social workers, child care workers and the Bishop of Stepney as to how homelessness and bad housing destroyed people, strained marriages, broke up families and stunted the development of children. The squatting families, suffering from all these ills, were thus driven by sheer necessity to occupy empty houses and commit what would otherwise have been wrongful acts. I should add that this was not a frivolous defence: 'necessity' is a recognized defence in law. We also filed evidence explaining how reasonable our demands were, that there were over *400 empty houses in Southwark that the council did not intend to use* and that we were not holding up the council's rehousing programme as we wanted to occupy houses only that would otherwise be left empty. We filed evidence too of how well the scheme worked in neighbouring Lewisham. The council were not expecting anything like this, and they themselves applied for an adjournment of the case on 21 October. The new date set was one week later, 28 October. Any delay helped the squatters, both because it gave them more time and also because every court hearing gave us further opportunities for demonstrations. A number of them had already been held, including a march to the Town Hall which was well supported by families from Lewisham.

The case was finally heard on 28 October. The squatters' legal case was argued by James Comyn, QC, and John Glidewell, QC appeared for the council. We lost, as I suppose we had expected, because even in our wildest dreams we could not see a court allowing families to squat. However we achieved what we wanted – a twenty-eight day order rather than an immediate one and, even more important, a further stay of execution if we appealed within twenty-one days. The hearing itself and our pickets of the High Court received national publicity; one newspaper even pictured a squatting child carrying a banner saying 'Southwark Council fights for the right to keep houses empty.' All the time we hammered out the message – Tory Lewisham lets squatters occupy empty houses, Labour Southwark evicts them.

The Southwark squatters formed themselves into a well-run organization, secured an office at the Union of Girls Schools

Settlement (U G S) and held meetings every Thursday. At these meetings policy and tactics were discussed, committee recommendations approved or rejected and action planned. The major need was recognized to be more families: everyone realized that the greater the number of squatters the stronger was the group's position; existing families organized and executed new squats and soon there were fifteen families in occupation. With 9,000 families on the council's waiting list and 4,500 of them in urgent need, it was not hard to find families who were forced to squat. Organizations and individuals throughout the borough were contacted and the extreme reasonableness of the squatters' case was stressed. The success of a similar scheme in Lewisham was also repeatedly pointed to. In this way opinion was gradually lined up against the council. Two local settlements, U G S and Cambridge House-Talbot Settlement came out publicly against the council. Another, Blackfriars Settlement, offered to try to settle the deadlock by mediation. The council rejected this outright and, on hearing this unofficially, the squatters announced their willingness to accept mediation. Even the *South London Press*, which had condemned the Lewisham arrangement back in 1969, had the grace to admit its mistake, and published two editorials calling on the council to commence negotiations and enter into a Lewisham-type scheme. The council, however, refused to move from its intransigent position and merely mouthed statements about the squatters holding up their 'patch-repair' programme, or not being on the housing list. These remarks, cunningly designed to appeal to people's parochial fears about 'outsiders taking their homes' were systematically replied to by the squatters. But at every opportunity the council tried to appeal to the lowest, irrational, parochial fears and prejudices of the Southwark residents.

Two particular acts by the council at the beginning of November demonstrate their fear of free and rational discussion on the matter and their worry at the increasing number of squatters. On 4 November at about 3 p.m. council workmen entered 14 Mortlock Gardens SE 15 and systematically smashed it to pieces – ripping out pipes and fittings, smashing the sink and toilet, ripping out the fireplace, taking up floorboards, removing windows and banisters. The house had been vacated only a few days earlier and we had seen that it was in good condition. It had a life of at least eighteen months and we had planned to use it. The council, however, preferred the Redbridge tactic of destroying good houses. In the weeks that followed this, dozens of other houses were similarly smashed by council workmen. Fortunately, the squatters learnt of the smashing of 14 Mortlock Gardens immediately, and were able to take photographs of the damage caused by the council. These were blown up and used in numerous pickets and marches in the future. The house wrecking incensed the families as well it might and the council's initial explanation – 'rat prevention' – served only to make them more annoyed.

The other high-handed act by the council concerned the Southwark Social Workers Lunch Club's invitation to me to address them on squatting. When the council heard of it they exerted pressure on the Lunch Club Committee to cancel the invitation. The excuse they gave was that some of those attending the meeting would be council employees and the council felt it did not want them to hear me as I was linked with a group that was involved in *sub judice* litigation with the council (as the squatters had announced their intention of appealing against the court decision of 21 October) and also because I might mention the cases in my speech. The fact that the meeting was a private one which took place in social workers' own time and on non-council property made no difference. Council employees were not to hear criticism of the council's policy and if the Lunch Club refused to cancel the invitation, all council employees would be barred from attending. The Lunch Club Committee, one member of which was Mr Mercer, Southwark Housing Manager, decided there-fore to give in to this pressure, to stifle free discussion; the invitation to me was withdrawn, and instead Shelter was asked to send a speaker. To his credit, John Willis, the Director designate, nominated Jim Radford, but he too was unaccept-able, so another was asked for, but John declared that Shelter would chose its speaker and if one was unacceptable, then no other would be sent. I, of course, reported all these events to the national press and the council was besieged with enquiries about their actions. A number of papers carried reports on the matter, and the whole issue of freedom of speech for social workers was opened up. The situation was electric and arguments raged back and forth. Finally the Southwark branch of the British Association of Social Workers decided to ask me to speak to them and on 12 November over 100 of them crowded into Cambridge House in Camberwell to hear me. I had agreed to outline the squatters' general case and not mention Southwark, but talk of the policies of a 'hypothetical' borough left no one in any doubt about which council I was referring to, and when the Lunch Club, despite Mr Mercer, re-invited me to speak to them on 3 December, the affair had really backfired on the council. Not only had their employees had the opportunity of hearing me speak twice, but the council had been publicly criticized for their attempts to frustrate free speech.

Meanwhile, deputations to the Town Hall and marches continued. All ways in which to publicize the matter were explored and used by the squatters. More families were installed and no court action could be taken against them until the appeals had been heard. The number of families and the public opposition to Southwark Council were increasing all the time. Morale among the families was high, despite attempts by some council social workers to persuade individual families to give up the struggle, the usual carrots and half promises being used to try to break the solidarity of the campaign. The families held firm, actively supported by a few helpers from other squatting groups or from the Borough Polytechnic and with the sympathy of a very wide section of people. The whole of the 'left', however, did nothing at all to help the families in their fight for homes for themselves and others.

The more respectable 'left' politicians also ignored the squatters' pleas for help; Michael Foot, for instance, never bothered to reply, former Housing Minister Anthony Greenwood (now Lord Greenwood) was 'unable' to help. The squatters realized as many other working people have realized before, that their main strength was their determination to fight and win, and that neither the 'left' politicians nor the 'left' revolutionaries were going to help.

This determination was given a tremendous boost when the squatters' appeals against the possession orders granted under Order 113 were finally heard in the Appeal Court on 15 and 16 December. The case was lost, but the sympathy of the judges and the publicity it received made it a loss in fine style. Lord Justice Edmund Davies even stated that he thought Southwark Council should enter into a similar 'admirable' arrangement to that with Lewisham Council. The families received another twenty-eight days' grace, which meant that they could not be finally evicted until the end of January. Order 113, the quick way to get rid of squatters, on which Southwark Council had relied so heavily, had enabled the council to evict squatters only after nearly five months!

Pressure on the council began to mount after the appeal hearing. Des Wilson and John Willis of Shelter wrote to the council supporting the squatters' case. The Bishop of Woolwich, the Rt Rev. David Sheppard, who lives in Peckham, led an all-denominational clerical deputation to see the council on Christmas Eve, and after these talks he issued a press statement, condemning the council's line, which received national publicity. The Family Squatting Advisory Service – the 'respectable' wing of the squatting movement[1] wrote asking if its representatives, Des Wilson, John Willis, Antony Fletcher (Quadrant Housing Association) and James Alexander (Trinity Housing Association) could meet the council. Leader John O'Grady saw no point in discussions. The Bishop of Stepney, Father Trevor Huddleston, Archbishop Roberts, Jeremy Thorpe, and many other 'weighty' figures wrote supporting the squatters. Just about everyone knowledgeable urged the council to back down, but to no avail. Southwark squatters' co-ordinator Barry Stone, and Bob Clayton who had been elected to do the job when Barry took a rest, continued to circularize people and organizations with information on the squatters' case. At the end of December, the squatters decided to send out a detailed rebuttal of every argument the council had ever put up against them. This went out on 29 December to every Southwark councillor, all chief officers, MPs, clergymen, the Department of the Environment, housing associations, local

1. See Chapter 11, page 178.

organizations and many people. It systematically destroyed the council's case[1] and resulted, at last, in some councillors expressing support for the squatters. At the council meeting on 6 January, there was, for the first time, open discussion on the issue, but the council's policy remained unchanged.

The court orders were due to expire in the middle of January 1971 but, over the weekend of 10th and 11th, the squatters commenced their evasion tactics, and three families vacated their houses and re-squatted in other properties. This meant that, after nearly five months, the council would have to start all over again. A few days later another family moved to avoid the court order.[2] The game of musical chairs had begun in earnest. Three more families were also on the point of moving when the council told them they could stay where they were until the houses were ready to be demolished. 'It seemed the most sensible thing,' said the council. Southwark squatters, of course, had been saying just that for four and a half months.

Alone among the left-wing politicians to respond to our appeal for help was Richard Marsh MP, Shadow Minister for the Environment. To his credit, he did involve himself, and on Monday 12 January he met Southwark chief executive Samuel Evans and council leader John O'Grady at Peckham Town Hall. He urged the council to compromise with the squatters and let the empty houses be used. An approach by the Shadow Minister, a senior member of their own party, was not something that could be shrugged off lightly and, as at the council meeting on 6 January, the council were obliged to produce information to justify their policies. Marsh had read the squatters' document of 29 December so rather more sophisticated arguments had to be relied upon. In the event, Marsh was told all about the council's patch repair policy and how

1. This rebuttal is reproduced in Appendix 2.
2. It is important to understand how this can be done under Order 113. The resulting eviction order is against all occupants, so the tactic adopted by the squatters was to vacate and move to a different house entirely. The council would then board up the previous one – officially repossessing it – and the squatters would move in another family (not the same one). The council would then have to start again.

fast they were implementing it.[1] There were only thirty-four houses that were uneconomic to patch repair – and they were the ones the squatters were so interested in; the council was, of course, quite prepared to allow a 'responsible housing association' to use them, but not the squatters. Richard Marsh was thus fobbed off with this explanation of the council's policy.[2]

The pressure on the council still continued though. Jeremy Thorpe MP brought the matter up in Parliament, and I have received information that two high-ranking officers from the Department of the Environment went to Southwark, only to receive the same curt answers as everybody else. More important people than all these, the squatters, despite a few casualties, continued to grow and the number of families in occupation crept up to twenty-five. This was clearly of vital importance, as, following the appeal, all the other suspended cases were heard and the council was, on every occasion, given twenty-eight-day possession orders. It was fundamentally important that the council should be shown that, far from being intimidated by this, the squatters were fighting on as determined as ever.

It was at this time that Antony Fletcher of Quadrant Housing Association became more involved. He drew up 'some proposals for the settlement of current difficulties' which he submitted to the squatters and the council. The reaction from the latter was abrupt – they were not interested. Thus, despite what had been said to Richard Marsh MP, the council was not interested in using a housing association to achieve a peaceful or compromise settlement.

In their press statement of 24 September, the council had explained that one of their reasons for rejecting the squatters' proposals was that they would involve the council sharing control of their housing estates with, of all things, people with an interest in the matter! Thus, the squatters could not use the vacant houses, and the only course was to leave them empty,

1. This was actually true: they were almost breaking their necks to get houses patch repaired. The squatters had at least produced that much effect.
2. The council's implementation of even this policy was, however, both grudging and derisory. Four houses had been handed over to Ladyholme, and three very poor ones to the South Bank Housing Society.

smash them up and evict those who dared to challenge the Labour council's doctrines. Another point that had enraged council leader John O'Grady in particular was that, as he said in an unpublished letter he wrote to *The Times* on 18 January, the squatters had occupied houses first and only sought negotiations afterwards. They had then gone outside the official channels and the fact that they were literally on the streets was no excuse. To the 'socialist minded' John O'Grady, ordinary working people acting for themselves just could not be allowed. To John O'Grady the squatters had committed the cardinal sin, that of going outside the normal channels.

Two factors then led, in January 1971, to a change of policy by the squatters. The first was the council's completely unyielding line and absolute refusal to accept any compromise solution. The second was the information about empty houses that the pressure had obliged the leader of the council and the chairman of the Housing Committee to provide. The squatters obtained highly confidential council documents which showed that their public statements were at variance with the facts. The decision facing the squatters was simply 'what should we do about this'. To publish the documents and accuse them of lying would entail a change from the 'ultra-reasonableness' policy, whereas not to publish would allow the council's public figures, which supported their case, to go uncorrected. It was, therefore, decided by the squatters to publish.

On 8 February, two days before the February meeting of Southwark Council, every councillor, alderman and chief officer received a document entitled 'Conspiracy to Deceive'. In this, council leader John O'Grady and Housing chairman Charles Sawyer were accused of making grossly misleading or inaccurate public statements. On 9 February, the squatters held a press conference publicly to accuse these councillors. In support of the squatters' claims, photostat copies of confidential council documents were handed out. In addition to showing that these two councillors had made inaccurate statements, one document in particular, a confidential report written by chief executive Samuel Evans on 30 November 1970, showed that of over 100 houses with over two years' life that the council had found uneconomic to patch repair, many were to be demolished years in advance of redevelopment, while the rest were to have all services stripped out. This secret and nasty policy of prior demolition and wrecking of houses with an *admitted* two years' life at least, incensed the squatting families who wished to see the places used rather than wasted. The council reacted immediately and called a press conference on 10 February, but this was cancelled at the last minute as the document had been referred to the council's lawyers for consideration. At the council meeting on 10 February, one councillor, Richard Percival, put down some questions about the document, but his (Conservative) party leader withdrew these for him on the grounds that the whole matter was *sub judice*, as the council's lawyers were considering the documents. About three weeks later it was announced that on counsel's advice there were good grounds for a libel action, but no action would be taken if the squatters stopped circulating 'Conspiracy to Deceive'. The squatters reacted by calling this bluff, and a further 100 copies were sent out. No public reply to the accusations had yet been given, and this surprised the squatters. This surprise was short-lived, for in March another confidential document came into the squatters' hands; Members Information Paper 13, dated 16 February. This purported to be a 'reply' to 'Conspiracy to Deceive' and was sent to council members only. Although it did probably answer one point raised in 'Conspiracy to Deceive', it had no answer to the major accusations.

At the council meeting on 17 March Councillor Percival's questions were at last allowed. But, despite the squatters' accusations, the statements by Councillor Sawyer and Councillor O'Grady continued to be grossly inaccurate. At one point Councillor O'Grady denied point blank that it was the council's policy to include properties that were uneconomic for them to patch repair in demolition contracts as soon as possible. In view of the chief executive's report of 30 November his denial is quite remarkable, as is the council's reply to the squatters' accusation. The libel threats had frightened no one and in furtherance of their new militant policy the squatters embarked on a series of demonstrations, to publicize their case even more. The first took place in the afternoon of 6 April

1971, when forty people descended on Peckham Town Hall and, after occupying the entrance hall, proceeded up to chief executive Samuel Evans's office. Mr Evans was amazed to see his office occupied by squatting families. 'Now tell us, face to face,' demanded Jean Fullerton, 'why can't we live in the houses you don't want to use. It's O K for you living in Orpington, but we've got nowhere to live.' 'I'm only an officer, I'm carrying out orders,' said Mr Evans. 'That's what Pontius Pilate said,' retorted someone. While this was going on other squatters were visiting every office in the building and distributing shortened and up-dated versions of 'Conspiracy to Deceive' entitled 'How do you like working for a dishonest boss?' This pointed out to the council staff how their employers, the leader of the council and the chairman of the Housing committee, had misled the public. The leaflet challenged them to sue the squatters for libel.[1] Eventually the police arrived on the scene, but to the annoyance of the council's senior officers, refused to remove the squatters. They saw their role as preventing breaches of the peace rather than intervening in civil disputes. They would arrest anyone who resisted in any way, but they would not remove the squatters. The council staff themselves were thus obliged to do the job and gradually the squatters were picked up and dumped outside the building, where the demonstration continued for another half an hour on the Town Hall steps.

Two days later, on 8 April, the day before Good Friday, staff at Castle House, the council's social services headquarters, also received the leaflets. The new militancy was beginning in earnest and, on 21 April, the squatters pulled off another coup. With the council meeting due to commence at 7 p.m., about fifty squatters decided that for once the truth about empty houses was going to be told in the council chamber and, at 6.30 p.m., the chamber was occupied and all doors fastened from the inside. With the official councillors thus locked out, the new 'councillors' conducted their 'council' meeting, and for over an hour nothing the council did could budge them.

1. In Appendix 1 I reproduce a detailed account of the lies of O'Grady and Sawyer. It is essential that this is read very carefully, so that the claims of the squatters in their two leaflets can be appreciated.

Eventually, police broke open the doors, and council leader John O'Grady entered the council chamber and tried to speak. After initially being ruled 'out of order' by the squatters' 'mayor', he was allowed to address the meeting. He consented to a meeting with the squatters' representatives and, as a result, after further discussion and a vote the squatters vacated the council chamber, with morale sky-high.

No one had any illusions about the meeting with the council and, as anticipated, it was a waste of time. The council simply repeated that they were not prepared to change their line and nothing could persuade them. Indeed the council had already prepared a press statement rejecting any settlement, in much the same way as before the very first discussions back in September.

Councillor O'Grady complained that the squatters had skilfully avoided all the council's legal processes, but asserted that eventually time would run out for them. Following the appeal in December and the expiration of the court orders in January, after completing all the suspended hearings in the High Court and obtaining twenty-eight-day orders in all cases, the council had, at the end of February, decided to switch to using the County Court, and seek possession under Order 26 Rule 6. This is the County Court equivalent to Order 113. The council's solicitor, Mr Millar, was expecting a short sharp hearing, but he was in for quite a shock.

We had managed to obtain a copy of the council's standing orders and it seemed from a close reading of these that the council had violated certain of their own procedural regulations in the way in which they had initiated legal proceedings against the squatters. For although the Housing (Urgency) Sub-Committee had authorized the proceedings to be taken, it seemed that the Finance Committee had not voted them the money to do it. Barrister Mr Frank Dorman argued on the squatters' behalf, therefore, that the council was wrongfully in court. After assistant Town Clerk Thomas Thomas was called to the witness box the council won the case, but the possession orders were suspended until the determination of an appeal if the squatters lodged it within twenty-eight days. This meant a further few months' delay and was important for the squatters as it gave them more time to get more families in occupation and gave the families some months 'security'. The number of squatting families was now nearing thirty, despite the fact that one or two had dropped out. The council would thus have a formidable task even when they did finally obtain more possession orders. In the event, an almighty oversight by the squatters nearly let the council off the hook – the appeal was not lodged within twenty-eight days, the suspension of possession orders ended and three families received bailiff's notices for evictions. In a panic the appeals were lodged and an application was made at the beginning of April to Lambeth County Court for the orders to be suspended until the appeal was heard. It was explained that a mistake had been made over the filing of the appeals. The judge, however, refused to suspend the orders until the appeal was determined, but he did suspend them for five days and said that if the squatters wanted the full suspension they would have to appeal direct to the Court of Appeal. It was two days before Easter, and the new suspension would end the day after the holiday. We rushed up to the High Court and filed an application for suspension next day, but the court had risen and all the judges had gone away. Somehow we had to get before a judge, and finally, after feverish activity, an emergency vacation hearing before an Appeal Court judge was arranged, and resulted in Lord Justice Karminski granting a suspension until the court re-convened properly. By a hair's breadth the squatters had wriggled out of trouble and two weeks later the Court of Appeal granted the suspension of the possession orders until the appeal was heard. It had been a near thing, however.

Following the occupation of the council chamber it was decided that the next step should be to present a petition to the council. This was signed by fifty-six social workers employed by them, condemning the council's anti-squatter policy and urging them to reach agreement with the squatters along Lewisham lines. The petition was presented to the council by fifty children of squatting families on 27 April, and the squatters' case was once again helped by the reaction of the council. In the next few days all the social workers were called to Peckham Town Hall and 'carpeted'. They were asked to withdraw, but none, so far as I know, did, at that time. Systematic leaks about these events kept them in the national press and the image was developed of a council pursuing a policy contrary to the opinion of its own employees.

The Southwark squat was developing nicely into an issue that the national press were keen to report, and it was important that this was continued. On Monday 10 May 1971, the next demonstration was held and it was specifically designed acutely to embarrass the Labour Council of Southwark just three days before the local elections on 13 May. At 2.45 p.m. two vans drew up outside Transport House, the national headquarters of the Labour Party and thirty people quickly got out, hurried into the building and proceeded to the first floor. After searching to find a suitable office – and nearly choosing the wrong one – the office of the assistant general secretary was entered. The clerical staff present were told they could either leave immediately or stay. They chose the latter and the doors were chained and wedged shut by Alf Williams of Abridge and Redbridge fame. A banner was unfurled out of the windows proclaiming that 'Labour Southwark Fight the Homeless'. Some of the occupiers made speeches from the windows to passersby using a megaphone. Outside more demonstrators gave out leaflets, while two more reached the roof of Transport House, unfurled another banner and showered leaflets to the street below. The occupation continued for an hour, until Labour Party general secretary Sir Harry Nicholas arrived, and phoned the squatters from the part of Transport House still in Labour Party hands. He agreed to meet the squatters, hear their evidence and investigate the goings-on in Southwark. The squatters then agreed to leave, and three went to see Sir Harry and promised to let him have all the necessary information.

On the same day as the occupation of Transport House the Family Squatting Advisory Service[1] held a press conference to

1. With Lewisham's success in rehousing families, Jim Radford thought that we ought to be able to get a grant from Shelter to help us spread the idea. Some people, myself very much included, were very dubious about this, thinking that such a grant could turn out to be a millstone round our necks. However, as we were going to try to stir things up elsewhere, and in order to do this full-time we had to have an income, there seemed no reason

report on its first six months' work. The F S A S could not be directly or officially involved in Southwark, but was extremely concerned at the number of empty houses in the borough. The FSAS had already become involved by seeking, unsuccessfully, a meeting with the council in December, and also because it was the F S A S who had asked Richard Marsh MP to approach Southwark Council. We considered that the best way in which we could assist the Southwark squatters was to isolate and encircle Southwark Council, and on 10 May our press conference reported our progress. Tower Hamlets had 'fallen' in January 1971 after a long struggle at Arbour House. An arrangement had also been reached with Greenwich via Quadrant Housing Association, and Camden was handing over houses to our group there. The long negotiations in Redbridge had resulted in Trinity Housing Association obtaining houses, and in Islington, Lambeth and Wandsworth squatting groups were negotiating with their councils. The Greater London Council was also handing over houses to a number of groups.

In Southwark, however, the council remained as entrenched as ever. On 12 May, just one day before the election, Southwark Council carried out its threat to apply for injunctions against squatting families. After their rude shock at Lambeth County Court and with those appeals still outstanding, Southwark Council decided to return to the High Court, and they applied again for possession under Order 113[1] and also for injunctions to restrain the squatters from occupying any other council property. These would, in theory anyway, have prevented families from re-squatting to thwart eviction orders. The council, however, received yet another legal set-back.

---

why Shelter, rather than the Lewisham families, should not support this. Jim therefore made tentative approaches to the then director of Shelter, Des Wilson, and Des, having got over his initial hostility towards the squatters, seemed prepared to help; he and director-designate John Willis, who took over in February 1971, recommended the idea to the Shelter trustees. A £5,000 grant was secured, and the Family Squatting Advisory Service was established on 1 December 1970, and I became its field officer and Anne Gross its secretary-field officer.

1. Having meanwhile passed the necessary resolutions to ensure that they were within standing orders.

They obtained twenty-eight-day possession orders without much difficulty, but Mr Justice Plowman explained that he could not grant the injunctions, as under Order 113 there was no provision for injunctions. The council had thus adopted the wrong procedure. Both evening papers on that day carried long stories about the Southwark squatting situation. The *Evening News* ran a feature on the squatters' new co-ordinator, Caroline Mayow. The *Evening Standard* reported the court hearing and Caroline's speech to the judge. On 13 May various daily papers carried reports of the court hearings and nicknamed Caroline 'the squatters' Portia'. Not only had the council received much adverse publicity, they had not even obtained their injunctions.

The squatters continued their campaign to publicize their case. A meeting was held outside 10 Downing Street, various moves were made to get Harold Wilson to intervene and 'discipline' O'Grady for non-Socialist policies. Needless to say the party leader took no action. The Labour Party while, no doubt, sympathizing with the homeless, was not prepared to act to stop its local council evicting them and leaving hundreds of usable houses empty. On 2 June, another council office was occupied – the homeless families department in Grove Lane, Camberwell. A leaflet – 'The Grief Report' – was distributed, which documented some of the homeless families' cases. The office was held for five hours and some families wanted to remain all night. After much discussion, however, it was finally decided to leave and save the 'all nighter' until next time. On 9 June the council's next batch of applications for possession orders (but no injunctions this time) came up, and Caroline Mayow again spoke for the squatters; Mr Justice Plowman granted a two-week adjournment to enable the squatters to apply for legal aid. This further delay greatly annoyed the council, and at one point during the hearing their barrister, opposing the adjournment, turned round to assistant Town Clerk Mr Thomas and exclaimed 'It's no good, he [the judge] won't listen to me, he only takes notice of her.'

On the appeals from the Lambeth County Court decision on the standing orders argument had been heard, and the council had won, and possession orders were granted. In addition the council did finally obtain injunctions restraining the families from continuing in unlawful occupation and also restraining them from occupying further houses, or any council offices. To do this they had to switch from using Order 113 in the Chancery Division to using the normal writ for possession and order for interim injunction in the Queens Bench Division. The disadvantage of this from the council's standpoint was that the speedy possession hearing under Order 113 was forsaken in return for the immediate injunction, although even this were suspended for twenty-eight days initially. This is almost unheard of – an interim injunction being suspended. If the families disobeyed the injunctions, the council remedy was not eviction but committal to prison for contempt of court. By the end of June then, after about ten months' of struggle, the council had finally got the squatters in its legal grip. Some had possession orders against them and others had injunctions. The squatters' usual process of moving to a new house to avoid the possession orders had been carried on since January and the injunctions were designed to stop this. The squatters, of course, decided to ignore the injunctions and Southwark Council were faced with the unpleasant choice that Hammersmith and Tower Hamlets had faced: they had either to jail homeless families, as Kent had done in 1965–6, or not enforce the injunctions. It must have been quite deflating for the hardliners on Southwark Council to realize that, although they had at long last won their legal battle, they still could not, in fact, stop the squatters. It was simply impossible for Southwark Council, a Labour council at that, after all the publicity, after all the squatters' logical argument and after all the squatters' calls for compromise, to enforce the injunctions; the council would have been torn apart, especially as, since the May elections, the Labour majority had increased and had resulted in the election of some Labour councillors sympathetic to the squatters. These would have called emergency council meetings, defied the party whips and even resigned.

Lambeth squatters meanwhile had, after a short struggle, reached an agreement with their council to take over empty houses. This received widespread publicity in south London, and it meant that Southwark was even more encircled than before. Southwark's position was completely impossible; they had finally, after ten months, secured a (legal) victory over the squatters which was more embarrassing for them than for their opponents. It was at this point that Councillor Sawyer let it be known unofficially that the council would not enforce the injunctions or any possession orders, and that he wanted a settlement. Eventually, in July or August, council leader O'Grady was reluctantly forced to accept the position.

While the struggle was at its height, the Southwark squatters had decided to hit the council on another front, and take them up on their public statements. The squatters decided that they would challenge the council's assertion that they were 'not a responsible organization' and try to gather together a really 'heavy' group of respectables to approach the council for the empty houses. It was thought that the increased militancy would make more and more councillors want a way out, and it was also thought that this met the council's only remaining objection to handing over the houses; if they still refused to do so the council could really be publicly exposed.

The Family Squatting Advisory Service, the 'respectable' non-direct action wing of the movement, was then asked to implement this policy. This became my job and it was no easy task. The FSAS itself could not carry out this role, as it (and the Lewisham group) had done in Tower Hamlets, because as far as Southwark Council was concerned Jim Radford and myself were tarred with the same brush as the Southwark Family Squatting Association. Furthermore, there were extreme dangers in this policy of setting up groups of 'heavy respectables'. They had to be weighty and moderate enough really to put the screws on the council and force them either to give in or be publicly exposed for not even dealing with a respectable group, but also they had to be sympathetic enough to the squatters to ensure that the interests and basic principles of the squatters were not forgotten. It would have been useless if this group had forced the council to hand over the houses, but then forgotten about the squatters; it would also have been useless even if the group had obtained the houses and rehoused the squatters but retained control itself in a paternalistic and authoritarian fashion.

With these considerations in mind I arranged for an informal discussion to set up this group on 8 April. I invited David Sheppard, Bishop of Woolwich, Sam Silkin, Labour MP for Dulwich, Des Wilson, ex-Director of Shelter, and Cecilia Goodenough of South Bank Housing Society.

With the exception of Des Wilson these people met on 8 April and agreed to set up a group to approach Southwark Council. They also accepted the principle of families' control – on this David Sheppard was vital to counter the ultra-legalistic and ponderous approach of Sam Silkin. It was agreed to call a larger meeting for 14 May to launch this group. On my suggestion they invited Ian Dixon of Co-ownership Development Society and Notting Hill Squatters, Antony Fletcher of Quadrant and a representative of Shelter, who because of their commitment to FSAS would go along with the principles of squatting. Sam Silkin suggested someone from Cambridge House-Talbot Settlement, where FSAS had its offices, and after a vociferous staff meeting there at which I described the purpose of the new group, Betty Roberts was chosen to represent them. Betty had signed the settlement's condemnation of the council back in 1970 so I knew her to be sympathetic to the squatters. It was important, if the tactic was to succeed, that the group should not appear to be picked by me or by the squatters as the council was to be given no excuse. Thus people like Don Phelan of Southwark Trades Council and Ron Watts and Evelyn Ackroyd, who had become Labour councillors a day before the meeting, on 13 May, were also invited. None of these were noted for their pro-squatter views, but provided they were prepared to go along with the idea of families' control of this new group when it was established, they were useful and even essential members of the group.

The group formed itself officially at the meeting of 14 May, and decided to make tentative approaches to the council. The Southwark squatters, knowing all this was going on, became doubly keen to keep up their militancy and the publicity. Clearly the council could not reject this group outright: the squatters' campaign, the council's own past statement and the 'respectability' of the group made such a course impossible. On the other hand the council knew that what this group was suggesting was *identical* to what the squatters had been suggesting since September 1970 – houses should be handed over and control should rest with the families. It was also made clear, to council leader John O'Grady at least, that the squatters would be rehoused quickly by this group and then would become a powerful section of its membership. On the one hand, rehousing the squatters was just what O'Grady and other hard-liners needed to get them out of a hole, but on the other it was the least acceptable solution, as it would give the squatters everything they had ever demanded.

Throughout May, June and July therefore, the policy group[1] of the Labour councillors was faced with this dilemma: they could not reject this group and they could not give in. They thus avoided making a decision and stalled as much as possible. Meanwhile the Labour group had terrific rows on the whole issue. Some councillors[2] were threatening to defy party discipline and even to sign resolutions to call emergency council meetings on the issue. It was towards the end of June, while all this was going on, that the council finally obtained its possession orders and injunctions. Thus, in addition to all the public pressure, any move to enforce them would have resulted in war inside the Labour group on Southwark Council.

It was at this point that housing chairman Charles Sawyer, who had been the first committee chairman to opt for a settlement, let it be known that no court orders or injunctions would be enforced while the negotiations were continuing. The quarrels within the Labour group had forced this concession from the hard-liners. The squatters decided to keep quiet and thus not give the hard-liners ammunition to use against those councillors who favoured a settlement. So the demonstrations were halted and throughout July the hard-liners stalled. O'Grady was wavering, but there were others far more anti-settlement than he. Among them were Councillor Kitty Clun (deputy leader), Councillor Halford (Planning Committee chairman), and Councillor Rev. John Watson (Social Services chairman).

1. i.e., the chairmen of committees plus the leader and deputy leader.
2. Particularly those newly elected on 13 May. The hard-line Bermondsey–Walworth group remained as intransigent as ever.

In addition chief executive Samuel Evans maintained his hard line. Gradually, however, these councillors became more and more isolated and the crunch came when the new group, which had called itself Southwark Self-Help Housing on the suggestion of Anne Ward,[1] became impatient. After one particular meeting with the Labour policy group in July, Sam Silkin wrote to the Council on behalf of Southwark Self-Help Housing giving them an ultimatum – agree by the beginning of August or he would issue a press statement attacking them.

Housing chairman Charles Sawyer was becoming increasingly confident of his ability to push the settlement through. The hard-liners were trapped. Chief executive Samuel Evans, whose first real stand on being appointed in 1970 had been against squatters, was 'taken off' squatting. Previously day-to-day handling of things had been almost entirely in his hands[2] but now Councillor Sawyer assumed control.

When the policy group met at the beginning of August a furious row took place, but finally Charles Sawyer and the pro-settlement side won: the 'inner cabinet' of Labour councillors became committed to a settlement, despite the opposition of Councillors Clun, Halford and the Rev. John Watson. Another hard-liner, Councillor Irene Thomas, the Chief Whip, left before a vote was taken.

Following this decision proper negotiations took place between Southwark Self-Help Housing and the council. These, however, were slowed down by the council bureaucracy, and also because during August and September a number of people involved were on holiday and the council itself was 'in vacation'. Despite all this, negotiations went ahead and by the middle of September were well advanced. The squatters, meanwhile, lived peacefully in their houses, ignoring both injunctions and possession orders.

However, there were still two battles to be won. The first arose because, although the policy group of Labour councillors

1. And with the support of the Southwark squatters.
2. 'However there is one thing about Southwark which outsiders learn fast. "If it's the squatters you want to talk about," everyone says, "then it's Mr Evans you'd better see".' Simon Jenkins, the *Evening Standard*, 26 January 1971.

had agreed to the settlement, the remainder had not. The second was perhaps even more vital to the squatters.

The 'weight' of the people involved had 'beaten' the council, but it was now crucial that Southwark Self-Help Housing did not become a 'Frankenstein's monster'. Two things were, therefore, necessary – that the 'weighty respectables' should fade out when the group got going and not try to run the whole thing paternalistically, and that the interests of the squatters were not ignored. Throughout September and October there were some intensive manoeuvrings on both these points. The squatters felt that one important way in which they could ensure that Southwark Self-Help Housing protected their interests was to have the right person employed by the group. Advertisements had been placed in *New Society* by Self-Help Housing for a field officer to organize the start of operations once the full Labour group had ratified the settlement. The squatters wanted their candidate chosen for the job, and as Caroline Mayow had decided to go to college, it was decided that Mary Wells, a former Southwark teacher, should apply.

The interviews were to take place on Monday 20 September. One good thing already established in Southwark Self-Help Housing was that any appointment would only be for three months, and then be subject to ratification or otherwise by a management committee elected by the families, who would be in occupation by then. Another comforting factor was that a number of pro-squatter people had got themselves onto the interviewing committee. There was good reason therefore to expect Mary Wells to be chosen for the job.

But these hopes did not materialize and she was not chosen. The pro-squatter people had had to back down in order to avoid a split in the group, when two people, Don Phelan and Evelyn Ackroyd, stood rigidly against her selection on the ground that it might prejudice the chances of the full Labour group ratifying the settlement. The group chose an unknown girl from Liverpool who was then offered the job. This caused uproar in the squatters' ranks, particularly as Mary had been told by David Sheppard that they considered her to be the best applicant but had thought it unwise to appoint her. Derek Hatton decided to go to Liverpool and 'nobble' the girl who

had got the job. The result was that she turned the job down –
Southwark Self-Help Housing had therefore to re-advertise
and Mary Wells could then apply again. The interviews were
scheduled to take place on 26 October – one day after the
meeting of the Labour group where the agreement would be
finally ratified – or rejected! Thus that argument for not employing Mary would clearly not apply. However, even before
this, at the Self-Help Housing meeting in October, a long discussion on the nature of the internal structure of the group
had taken place, and mainly due to a speech by Ian Dixon the
'heavies' agreed that as soon as families were in occupation
they would hand over to them completely. An attempt by Don
Phelan to put the 'heavies' in a 'school governor' role was
defeated. It was also agreed that at the next interview ability
only would be considered. This was tantamount to agreeing
to employ Mary Wells, for there was no one else who was
going to apply with as much experience in the field. Indeed,
hints were dropped that the group hoped that Mary would
apply. Naturally she did just that and was appointed on 26
October and asked to start on 1 November.

On 25 October, the Labour group of the council had met.
Councillor O'Grady had neatly side-stepped an attempt by
Councillor Coombes to challenge the settlement, by claiming
that nothing had really been agreed! Whatever the official
position was, or whatever the internal workings of Southwark
Council, it was of no account. The squatters had discovered
that a meeting of the Housing (Urgency) Sub-Committee had
agreed to hand over the first thirty houses. Official, unofficial,
technical or otherwise, it was of no consequence: if the council handed over the houses *that* was what the squatters wanted.

On 1 November 1971, Mary Wells started work as field officer
for Southwark Self-Help Housing, and the first thirty houses
were handed over. After fourteen months of struggle Southwark Council had been beaten.

11. The FSAS and the Growth of the Movement

The idea of the Family Squatting Advisory Service was that it should eventually consist of representatives from all the local groups, but as in December 1970 there were not many of these, this was clearly not possible, so various interested and sympathetic people were invited to join. As more squatting groups have been formed these have elected representatives to FSAS and some of the interested sympathizers have dropped out so that now the FSAS committee consists almost entirely of the group representatives.

I have already described the role that the FSAS inherited in Tower Hamlets and Southwark. In addition to this, other groups sprang up in Greenwich, Lambeth, Wandsworth, Redbridge, Brent, Islington, Ealing and Waltham Forest, and an already-existing group in Camden joined with this developing movement. The birth of Greenwich lies in the Lewisham squatters. In summer 1969 while I was still at Lewisham, I had, with the assistance of Antony Fletcher, persuaded a reluctant Housing Manager Mr Gray to let me have a house in which to rehouse a homeless family. This broke our normal rule not to rehouse literally homeless families as these were the responsibility of the homeless families department, but it seemed a way of getting a foot in Greenwich. Developments in Greenwich however were slow but they received another boost when, early in 1971, two old blocks of flats in Woolwich, York and Lancaster Houses, were rejected by Quadrant for short-term use. These were passed to the squatters by Quadrant with the agreement of Mr Gray, and the Greenwich Family Squatting Association was formed. This arrangement, whereby the squatters received houses indirectly, was fair enough as a starting point, but was too unwieldy to be satisfactory on a permanent basis. Approaches were made to the council for a more direct arrangement, rather than that whereby officially the council gave the houses to Quadrant who passed them on to the squatters. The Labour Party which came to power in May 1971 was more sympathetic to the squatters than their Tory predecessors. An approach was made to establish a direct arrangement and, after a number of discussions and meetings, the arrangement was finalized in October, and nearly forty families have now been squatted.

Moves to start a group in Brent had also begun in 1970. As a result of an advertisement placed in *Time Out* by John Guy, a group was formed calling itself Brent Homeless Families. John Guy contacted people throughout the borough, and soon badly housed people from Willesden were joining the group. Negotiations were held with Tory housing chairman, Alderman Francis Pratt, and both he and council leader, Alderman Lee, made sympathetic public noises. But an agreement without a struggle with the Brent Tories was just too much to hope for, and despite all their public statements, they refused to play ball. The group had however already obtained the public support of the Labour minority, and if they won the forthcoming election they would find it hard to back down. This proved to be the case, and when Labour replaced the Tories after May they were committed to handing over the first twelve houses. But if the Labour Party could not back down, they could certainly try to attach oppressive conditions to any agreement, and this they did. They wanted to 'nominate' families for the houses; they wanted Brent Homeless Families to arrange permanent rehousing for the families when their short-life houses came down *before* they actually took up occupation. Hard negotiating ensured that the group kept its independence and obtained a similar arrangement as existed in other boroughs. This has now been achieved and the group has rehoused a dozen families.

Squatting in Lambeth began at the end of April when Chris and Pam Brown and their children occupied a house in Norwood. They looked round for support in the borough, other families were contacted, and soon there were five squatting families. An awkward situation then arose in Lambeth – families from the council's own welfare accommodation wanted to

squat. This was a problem as, compared with Lewisham,
Lambeth's temporary accommodation is appalling – and to
refuse to help families from one unit in particular, Louise
Court, was difficult as conditions were so bad. On the other
hand the council should not be allowed to palm off its responsibilities onto the squatters, so the group decided that it
should help the families in Louise Court to organize a tenants'
action committee to fight for improvements, speedy rehousing
and the closing down of Louise Court. A number of meetings
were held and a charter of demands drawn up and sent to
the council. The campaign is still going on but an immediate
result at least was that many outstanding repairs were
done.

In the Borough of Camden a group approached the council
towards the end of 1970 demanding the right to use short-life
properties, and received a satisfactory reply. This group –
Student Community Housing – is somewhat different from
most local groups both in name and function. Houses with
only three months' life are used, divided into rooms and used
to accommodate students. Recent articles in the national press
have shown that this section of society is also experiencing
increasing difficulty in finding accommodation. Student Community Housing is one practical way in which self-help can be
useful in this field. The group also obtains properties with a
longer life and these are used for badly housed or homeless
families. SCH has therefore affiliated to the Family Squatting
Advisory Service, and some of its members have been active in
assisting the formation of the Islington group. Perhaps one of
the best features of this group is the linking up of the problems
of two very different sections of society. Student Community
Housing has shown how badly housed families and students
can work together and as a result of this co-operation some
forty families and nearly two hundred students have been rehoused.

A similar group also developed at Crystal Palace in autumn
1971 when the GLC offered the FSAS six enormous twelve-
roomed Victorian houses standing in their own grounds with
at least five years' life. The snag was that the houses were in
the most appalling condition and the previous owners had sold

them to the GLC rather than face the repair bills. For any one squatting group to have taken on the Herculean task of renovating these houses would have been impossible so the Crystal Palace Project was formed. This consists of a group of architectural students – some married with children – who wish to live on part of the premises but who will also rehouse badly housed families who wish to join the project. By approaching the task in a communal way two of the houses have been rendered fit for habitation already and a number of families have been housed in emergency situations. On another of the houses the architects are proposing to try out various techniques of roofing which, if successful, could help other squatting groups by providing a speedy and cheap way of repairing roofs. The results of the Crystal Palace Project could thus greatly assist other groups and enable them to use even those houses previously rejected as unusable.

The London Borough of Ealing first saw squatters at the beginning of May 1971. The housing policy of the then Conservative council had been appalling – house building had been drastically reduced while the borough's policy on the homeless was even worse: the number of units of temporary accommodation was far too small and many families were turned away. Others were put up in bed-and-breakfast places where they remained for weeks on end. The regulations in these often meant that the family had to be out by 9 a.m. and not come back until 5 p.m. – no joke when there are children involved. Hand-in-hand with this policy went that of leaving houses empty, and one particularly bad area for this was Western Road, W5, near the centre of Ealing. The council had conceived a large-scale Ealing town centre redevelopment plan, with a ring road, shopping precincts and car parks. Although there had been no public inquiry, planning permission had not been granted and compulsory purchase orders had not even been issued, let alone approved, the council had begun acquiring houses well in advance of the implementation of the plan, and boarding them up – after the manner of Redbridge Council before the battles in 1969. Thus the houses in and around Western Road were scheduled to remain empty for at least two years.

At the beginning of May, Pat Valima and his wife and two children moved into one of the houses in Western Road. Pat had been the victim of another facet of Ealing's housing policy whereby people with a certain income were removed from the normal housing list and put on the 'deferred list' which meant that they would not be offered a council house, however desperate they were, but would instead be considered for a council mortgage. But when Pat Valima applied for a mortgage he was offered, on the basis of his income, the pitiful sum of £2,100. As there are no houses for sale at this price and as he stood no chance of getting a council house, despite being in desperate circumstances and having lived in Ealing for years, he and his family squatted. With the local elections only about a week away the Tory council took no action. After the local elections the Labour Party was returned and they were confronted with the problem. Two other families – the Moles and the Whites – followed the Valimas and squatted in Western Road while the council was still discussing its whole housing and homeless policy.

All three families then got busy gaining support and publicity. Pat Valima in particular contacted local organizations – the Ealing Communist Party, the Cuckoo Estate Tenants Association and others. He also contacted the Family Squatting Advisory Service and all three families expressed the wish to form a squatting group to persuade Ealing council to hand over more of its empty properties. Eventually, on 14 June, Pat Valima, Tony White and I met the council – leader Councillor Telfer, Housing chairman Councillor Dr Feldman, social services chairman Councillor Mrs Lord and various officers. We explained how the squatting scheme worked and asked what the council proposed to do with the current squatters. On this latter point no reply was forthcoming but on the wider issue of the empty houses the council informed us that they were disgusted at the 'bed-and-breakfast' practice and they were proposing to use a number of the short-life houses themselves.

The squatters continued to contact local organizations and the result was that on 27 July the Ealing Shelter group, Ealing Trades Council and the Cuckoo Estate Tenants Association called a public meeting at Ealing Town Hall to discuss home-

lessness in the borough and what could be done about it. I was
the main speaker and the meeting went very well, despite the
fact that I was at first continually heckled by some residents of
Western Road who were annoyed that I was not a councillor
to whom they could complain about the lack of information
they had as to when their homes were to be demolished. Some
walked out but over a hundred people stayed and decided to
form an Ealing squatting group; a committee was elected and
appointed to organize things and to do the ground work. This
committee consisted of all three squatters plus representatives
from the Trades Council, the Tenants Association and other
local organizations. A week later the committee met and
formed the Ealing Family Squatting Association. A letter to
the council was sent off explaining that the group wanted
to use the empty houses and asking for a meeting with the
council.

The council replied initially by holding informal discussions
and later by agreeing in principle to co-operate with the squatters. After some delay the first houses were handed over in
November. As the three original squatters in Western Road
had, by that time, been given rent books, squatting in Ealing
had been entirely successful.

And so the squatting movement continues. There have been,
it is true, some changes since those early days in Redbridge,
but the basic points remain – no council has the right to keep
houses empty for long periods, and ordinary badly housed
working people have the right to occupy them. In addition,
control of the operations is in the hands of the families themselves. I have not described the internal workings of each
group as they are all very similar to that of Lewisham. Naturally different groups solve problems in different ways, but the
ways in which decisions are reached are the same.

With some thirteen groups now organized and having representatives on the Family Squatting Advisory Service the possibility of wider action is now present. We have so far concentrated on establishing more groups and servicing and advising
the existing ones: now we can concentrate also on getting
them to push together for other demands.

12. Effects

Although they were never stated as such, the squatters movement started off with four aims. One of the chief aims of those
who started the movement was to spark off large-scale direct
action similar to that of 1946. Unfortunately, the hoped-for
self-activity of hundreds and thousands of people just did not
occur. Fear, alienation, conditioned acceptance of imposed
values all prevented this, and our initiative could not break
through all these in enough people quickly enough. However,
there have been occasions when families have squatted quietly
and entirely on their own in many places.

Early in 1969 there were some indications that homeless
people were going to be moved to action. On 15 February, only
a week after our initial squat in Ilford, three women and their
families occupied a council house in Winnersh, Berkshire,
just outside Reading. They acted entirely on their own
initiative and it was only after their initial occupation that the
militants from Reading arrived to help them. The women were
successful since, although they were evicted three days later,
they were immediately rehoused.

A couple squatted spontaneously in Leyton in February
1969 and defeated attempts to evict them. About the same time
a family in Stoke Newington moved into an empty house on
the same street as the house in which they had lived before it
was gutted by fire. Having lived in the road for many years
they had the support of all the neighbours; so much so that
when a private bailiff arrived at the house muttering threats
about eviction he was beaten off by an elderly resident armed
with a walking stick. Eventually they were offered accommodation by Hackney Council.

Further spontaneous squats occurred in Woodford, in Edin-
burgh, at the beginning of the long struggle in Southwark, in

Ealing, Hackney and Stoke, and many other isolated examples too numerous to mention in detail and which I only heard about at second hand. Although mass squatting has not occurred, the number of families that have squatted on their own over the last few years has certainly run into many hundreds. Some are short lived, some are successful, others result in court orders or evictions. On the other occasion when we might have gained the publicity to spread the movement within hostels, the authorities, realizing the potential danger, prevented the development of a squatting movement at the hostels concerned by granting considerable concessions and speeding up the rehousing of families.

However, the tactics of the campaign were sound. By publicizing squatting and securing gains we demonstrated one main thing – squatting works. Unfortunately, although the publicity arising from the Redbridge situation certainly had excellent effects on other local authorities the stories of evictions could well have deterred other families from squatting. Had our successes been plastered over the front page of the newspapers the results might perhaps have been very different.

With our second aim, that of achieving better housing by means of direct action, we have been more successful. When councils have been reasonable we have reached agreements, as in the case of Lambeth. There, after several squats, the Lambeth Family Squatting Association was formed and the usual demands were put to the council that the families should be allowed to stay and that other empty houses should be handed over to the squatters. The council appeared reasonable but tempers were frayed when, in June 1971, council workmen smashed up the interiors of two houses in Waylett Street in Norwood, ten minutes after they had been emptied. For a few days things seemed to be going the way of neighbouring Southwark. However, Housing vice-chairman Councillor Ken Livingstone was quick to point out that this wrecking was a mistake and he assured everyone that it was not council policy. An agreement was reached – the council was prepared to hand over short-life houses to the squatters, and as a result there are now over fifty families squatting in Lambeth.

The effects of the squatters campaign on local councils and

their empty property policies however were not confined simply to families that took part in the campaigns. The big confrontation with the authorities at King Hill Hostel, back in
1965–6, resulted both in widespread changes in hostel rules and
in other authorities being so afraid of that kind of confrontation that they gave in immediately (as at Abridge for instance).
Similarly the big confrontation in Redbridge which resulted in
that council being forced to make concessions and use at least
some of its empty houses, also had the result that other local
councils were wary of similar events in their boroughs. This
did not mean that any group, however disorganized, could defeat a local authority merely by arranging a squat, but it did
mean that any campaign that showed that it was well organized, determined and capable of both sustained struggle and
reasoned argument in public was probably going to meet with
considerable success relatively quickly. Even the GLC, which
many people in the squatters movement considered was the big
nut to crack after Redbridge, has changed its mind on its thousands of empty properties awaiting redevelopment. On the
'Man Alive' television programme in March 1969 Mr Horace
Cutler had publicly rejected a call from Jim Radford and me to
utilize these houses, but by 10 October of the same year he was
announcing that 2,000 of the GLC's empty properties were
going to be used. The *Observer* of 12 October disclosed that it
was a squat in Gomm Road, Southwark, that had been one of
the main factors in bringing about the GLC's decision.

The result of this decision has been that over a thousand
houses have been opened up all over London. Many have been
handed over to squatters in a number of boroughs. Family
Housing Association has obtained about 500 houses from the
GLC and they readily admit that this is thanks to squatting.
Quadrant Housing Association, Trinity Housing Association,
New Islington and Hackney Housing Association and dozens
more have received houses from the GLC in which they have
rehoused families. Many thousands have been rehoused as a
result of this GLC decision brought about by the squatting
movement.

The struggle in Redbridge reached such proportions and
such a level of national publicity that it even forced the

government's hand. In June 1969 a circular was sent to all local authorities by the Ministry of Housing urging them to use all properties in reasonable repair and with a life of two years or over; it also urged them to hand over to housing associations property with a life of less than two years. That the Ministry was prepared to give its recommendation some teeth was shown by the fact that in August 1969 Redbridge Council minutes show that the Ministry will not give that council loan sanction to buy houses for the second stage of its proposed redevelopment plan, unless the council guarantees to use the properties for housing purposes. Redbridge Council will thus never again get away with wrecking a house not required for six to eight years as it did with 43 Cleveland Road.

With concessions extracted from Redbridge and with Lewisham deciding to co-operate with the squatters, a number of people in the movement really felt that a vigorous propaganda campaign, plus a few more quick, successful struggles, could well have had the desired effect of spreading squatting. Then a series of events occured which changed the whole public image of the word 'squatter'. The London Street Commune occupied 144 Piccadilly, and a school in Endell Street, W1, among other places. The opinions of the members of the squatters campaign on these events were many and varied. 'Officially' of course the movement had no opinion as the two campaigns were quite separate, but individuals naturally held their own views. These ranged from being totally opposed to the London Street Commune to having some sympathy with it. One effect was that some squatters visiting families had to stress that they were not from the London Street Commune. I think it is also undeniable that the activities of the commune brought out the most reactionary feelings in many people who were prepared to allow the authorities to get away with murder in their dealings with young people. I think it is a fair conclusion to say that the dramatic occupations of 144 Piccadilly, the Endell Street school and other places were a factor which tended to hinder the development of a mass squatting campaign among the working class.

The publicity resulting from the Southwark squat probably

had a great influence on the numerous other councils that now hand over houses to the squatters. Lambeth Council are to close their hostels and use short-life houses instead; in Waltham Forest and Havering the use of Suttons Hostel has ended, and short-life houses are used there too; even in Lewisham when the Labour Party regained control and wanted to phase out the squatters they had to justify this by claiming that they were going to use the houses themselves. All over London the process has been the same – the old hostels are gradually being closed down and more and more short-life houses are being used by councils and handed over to squatting groups.

It is very difficult to judge how far the movement has succeeded in furthering the third aim, that of radicalizing attitudes to housing, but some tentative assessment can be made. One fact at least has given everybody involved in housing a boost, and the authorities a jolt. I think now, as I thought when squatting started, that housing is a key issue on which ordinary people can successfully fight the authorities, and it can be said that there has been a trend towards grass roots activity, to some extent caused by the movement. Ordinary working-class people are developing their own movements outside the normal party political (non) channels. In this development lies the hope for future increased militant action. Many people, who previously would not have thought of squatting as a tactic, now consider it viable. In Barnet, in 1969, a residents organization formed to fight a redevelopment plan at Cromwell Road in the borough. Briefly the situation was that the local council decided to redevelop the area, and so demolish a fairly large number of houses. The residents were opposed to this, campaigned against the plan and recommended other parts of their borough where the plan could be implemented without demolishing people's homes. The council discounted their protests and proceeded to buy up houses and to leave them empty. The residents, angered, both because they did not like to see good houses standing empty and because they knew that they would be next on the list, approached us in east London and asked us to squat in the houses. We were not able to do this as we were more than fully occupied in Ilford, but the approach is of some significance.

In 1969 a similar approach was made to us by a member of the Basildon Council minority Labour group. The group had some complaints against the Basildon Development Corporation which administered most of the houses in Basildon new town. Like all new town development corporations it was appointed and not elected so the local people had no control over it, even in theory. In August then the Labour group on the council approached us and suggested that we squat in some empty properties owned by the development corporation. Again we were unable to do this, but again this shows that the squatters movement has radicalized the kind of action considered possible by a very wide variety of people concerned with widely differing campaigns in the housing field. From considering such militant action to taking it, of course, is another step but at least the idea is now there.

Probably the most important development of the squatting movement is that working people have taken control of their own lives, to a small extent at least. In a dozen or more London boroughs working-class families control their own housing groups and the long process of conditioning that has made the downtrodden and pushed-around people reluctant to accept responsibility is being gradually broken down. Hopefully the non-squatting activists have learnt from the mistakes they made in Lewisham.

Clearly the involvement of more and more families must be continued – not so much by the non-squatting activists as by the active families, and also clearly the number of squatting groups must be increased until all or most London boroughs are covered.

The system typified by large empty office blocks is a good target for squatters. While land values increase because of property speculation, councils are hamstrung in any attempt to acquire land for housing, and while interest rates continue to rise, councils continue to have to pay out enormous sums to borrow money to finance house building. Even the most willing council in the world is therefore at the mercy of this system of private speculation, private money lending and property developing.

Private developers who build luxury flats and office blocks while people go homeless are also a possible target. So, too, are the councils which build houses at unsubsidized rents which result, in some areas, in new council houses standing empty for years because the rents are too high for those who need them.

It is essential for the squatting groups to fight these injustices and develop an allegiance to a wider movement, and this has already started. On 14 November 1971 all the groups held a conference at The Albany in Deptford. Over a hundred people attended, most of them being squatting families who did most of the talking. The principal point of the conference was to assist in the development of a feeling of a wide movement. Squatting groups, like all other groups, have their inward-looking parochial tendencies as well as their outward-looking progressive tendencies. The purpose of the conference, called and financed by the Family Squatting Advisory Service, was to encourage and increase the latter. It was successful in starting the process: most of the people present wanted more conferences and called for them every two or three months. The first step towards a wider movement was thus taken.

Thus one aim is this development: there is now some prospect that the squatting movement, having spent some time consolidating its position, could begin to act as a national force, and that in future the sections of society most affected by the housing situation – the badly housed and the homeless – will be the basis for a new radical housing movement.

Appendix 1
Councillors O'Grady and Sawyer

On 9 February 1971 the Southwark Family Squatting Association held a press conference to launch a document entitled 'Conspiracy to Deceive' in which two senior members of the Southwark Council – leader John O'Grady and housing chairman Charles Sawyer – were accused of public lying and deception, and called upon to resign. The council immediately sought legal advice and announced some two weeks later that although counsel had advised that they had good grounds for a libel action, no writs would be issued if the squatters refrained from circulating the document. The squatters continued to distribute it and indeed, on 6 April, published an abbreviated version entitled 'How do you like working for a dishonest boss?' which was circulated to council staff. This openly challenged the council to sue them, but no action has yet been taken.

It is my opinion that these two councillors did not sue simply because the accusations against them made by the squatters were correct. Furthermore, I maintain that even since the publication of 'Conspiracy to Deceive' statements have been made in the council chamber by Councillors O'Grady and Sawyer that are, to say the least, questionable when one considers the facts.

The dispute between the council and the squatters dates back to September 1970 when two families occupied houses in Harders Road, Peckham, SE 15. The Southwark Family Squatting Association was formed and approached the council with proposals that a similar scheme should be adopted in Southwark as had been operating successfully in neighbouring Lewisham.

Briefly the arrangement there is that the council allows the squatters to occupy houses awaiting redevelopment that it cannot use itself and which have a life of a year or more. In return the squatters agree to rehouse only Lewisham families, to vacate when the times comes for redevelopment, to arrange for their own rehousing at this time if they have not come up on the housing list and to do all their own repairs, thus incurring the council no expense. This scheme has worked and 200 families have been rehoused.

In addition the squatters have honoured their agreement and vacated houses when required to – the most impressive example of this has been the clearing of thirty-seven houses in the Adolphus Street site in Deptford on time. Redevelopment plans have not been held up by squatters.

Southwark Council, however, decided that they did not want squatters in the borough, and announced, at a press conference on 24 September 1970, that legal action to evict them – there were five families by this time – would be taken. A statement was issued outlining the council's reasons for this decision. The operation of a Lewisham-type scheme in Southwark would, it was claimed, attract outsiders to the borough, increase the number of families applying for welfare accomodation, result in families jumping the housing queue and delay the council's housing programme.

In addition the council announced plans to spend more money themselves on their short-life houses, and thus a survey was initi- ated of all fit properties with at least two years' life (houses with less than two years were not considered) with a view to patch repairing them where it was economic to do so.

The squatters announced their support for this but asked to be allowed to utilize those houses that the council still found un- economic to patch repair even within their new cost limits. The squatters also pointed out that the council's objections to their scheme were invalid – and pointed to Lewisham to support their case. Court proceedings were, however, commenced, which did not end until the middle of December. By this time more families had been 'squatted' and support for the squatters had grown. Even Lord Justice Edmund Davies, in the Court of Appeal, expressed the hope that the council and the squatters would reach an agreement similar to the 'admirable' one existing in Lewisham.

This advice was ignored by the council, and the conflict continued. As fast as the council obtained eviction orders, the families moved elsewhere and new families were moved in – until there were over thirty. The council then sought injunctions to stop all this and the squatters replied with numerous demonstrations, and a great deal of propaganda.

On 29 December 1970 they issued a six-page press statement which answered in great detail all the council's objections to a Lewisham- type arrangement. (This was even admitted by some councillors who now support the squatters.) It was at this stage that the leader of the council and chairman of the Housing Committee on Southwark Council, rather than answer the squatters' case, started to deceive and mislead the public. Even questions in the council chamber were not answered truthfully by them. Having lost the argument they thus resorted to lying about the empty properties, and the use to which they were going to be put (or not put).

Public Information v. Private Information

The council's survey of all fit properties with at least two years' life was proceeding, and a number of houses were being patch repaired by the council. Until 6 January 1971 however no information was available to the public on the number of empty houses and, more important, on the number the council had found uneconomic to patch repair. (It is these houses, of course, that the squatters wanted to use.) On that day, though, Southwark Council met, and following the squatters' press statement Housing chairman Charles Sawyer was questioned on the use of empty properties.

Councillor Hoskins asked him to state '(a) the total number of empty properties,' and '(b) the number of empty properties which cannot be used for any purpose,' (Minutes of Proceedings, page 303). Councillor Sawyer's reply was: '(a) the total number of acquired empty properties (including those which have been declared unfit for human habitation and those which are awaiting early demolition) is 1,626,' and '(b) approximately 1,200 of these properties are held for demolition and this figure includes properties which have been declared unfit for human habitation. The remainder will be patch repaired or converted,' (ibid. page 303).

The meaning of this is quite clear: of the 1,626 empty properties, about 1,200 either were due to be demolished or were unfit and so could not be used by anyone, while the remainder (i.e., those fit properties with two years' life or more which the council had decided to re-survey) 'will be patch repaired or converted'. Thus, there were no properties free for the squatters, anyway!

Councillor Sawyer's figures however are extremely difficult to reconcile with what *he knew* the facts to be – and it is worth remembering that notice is given of council questions so that the relevant chairmen can obtain the correct facts.

The council's survey of properties was well under way by January and, indeed, by 11 November 1970 when the Housing and Highways and Works (Building Contracts) Joint Sub-committee met it was reported that ninety-seven properties had been 'reinspected and found to be uneconomic to patch' repair (Document HSG 34.70–71, signed C. A. Halford, chairman). Councillor Sawyer was present at this meeting and so knew that ninety-seven of his 'remainder' that he claimed 'will be patch repaired or converted' were in fact 'uneconomic to patch'.

Further, on 30 November the council's chief executive, Mr Samuel Evans, reported that by then 'more than 100 properties already surveyed have been found to be uneconomic to patch repair within the new cost limits. It is estimated that the final number of such "uneconomic to repair" properties will be about 130,' (Document HSG 39. 70–71, confidential, 30 November 1970). Both this document and the other one referred to were on the agenda for the information of the full Housing Committee which met on 9 December and was chaired by Councillor Sawyer.

Thus when Councillor Sawyer told Councillor Hoskins in the council chamber on 6 January that the 'remainder will be patch repaired or converted' he knew that of this 'remainder' certainly 'more than 100' and an 'estimated' 130 were 'uneconomic to patch repair'. He also knew what was to happen to these properties. The chief executive's report of 30 November stated that although they 'are not within the immediate demolition programme ... steps are being taken to demolish them. A large number however are ... within future development areas and in these cases the only effective action ... is to strip out all services and board up, pending redevelopments.'

He also had in his possession the agenda (confidential) of the Housing (Management) Sub-committee meeting to be held on 7 January 1971 (the day after the council meeting). The agenda, however, was circulated on 1 January, so Councillor Sawyer had a copy by the 6th. In this agenda is a report from the property surveyor in which the addresses of 109 properties 'reinspected and found to be uneconomic' and the addresses of three more 'permanently boarded up' are listed (Document HSG/MAN 15. 70-71, dated 30 November 1970).

Thus Councillor Sawyer's public statement on 6 January is completely at variance with all the facts he had in his possession. When he said that 'the remainder will be patch repaired or converted' he did not tell the truth. This was the accusation of lying made by the squatters in 'Conspiracy to Deceive' published on 9 February.

It may perhaps be argued on Councillor Sawyer's behalf that he was including the 'estimated' 130 uneconomic to patch repair properties in the 1,200 that he told Councillor Hoskins were being held for demolition, and not in his 'remainder' and that, therefore, all of his 'remainder' were going to be used. Such an argument does not hold water. On 18 January Councillor John O'Grady wrote to *The Times*. Although unpublished this letter was issued to council mem-

bers and staff (i.e. not confidential) as Members Information Paper
no. 10. This states that 'about 1,300 properties are awaiting demolition in 1971'. When the squatters commented on this rise of 100
in 'Conspiracy to Deceive' the council explained it by saying that
eighty-five properties 'unsuitable for patch repair' had been 'earmarked ... for early demolition', and thus 'approximately 1,200'
on 6 January had risen to 'about 1,300' on the 18th. (Members Information Paper no. 13, confidential, 16 February 1971). In addition,
this confidential information paper says that forty-four more
properties had been found to be uneconomic to patch repair, making
a total of 129 – or, as Mr Evans had said back in November, an
'estimated' 130.

Now it must be admitted that this earmarking of eighty-five
houses for demolition does explain why the number held for demolition rose from 'approximately 1,200' to 'about 1,300'. In doing so
however, and in mentioning the other forty-four 'uneconomic to
repair properties' it also shows that these 129 properties were *not*
included in Councillor Sawyer's '1,200 held for demolition' but were
in fact included in his 'remainder' that 'will be patch repaired or
converted' but which he knew would not be, and instead would be
'earmarked for early demolition' or 'stripped ... of all services.'

Misleading Information

Councillor Richard Percival also questioned Councillor Sawyer at
the council meeting on 6 January. He wanted to know whether it
was true, as the squatters claimed, that the council had destroyed
the interior of 14 Mortlock Gardens, SE 15, in the Cossall Street
redevelopment site. Councillor Sawyer replied that 'the Council's
contractor has stripped out the interior of 14 Mortlock Gardens to
prevent its occupation by unauthorized persons as a demolition
contract on the Cossall Street area is due to commence in April or
May of this year' (Minutes of proceedings, page 304). Therefore
the house had too short a life to be used.

In 'Conspiracy to Deceive' the squatters argued that although
the demolition of one part of the Cossall Street site was due to start
in April 1971 (that is the Sunwell Street/Hooks Road 'unfit' part
of the site), the demolition of the site as a whole was not due to
finish until September 1972 (information obtained from Planning
Department) and that the demolition of Mortlock Gardens was not
due to start until well into 1972 – particularly as the compulsory
purchase order on that part of the site had not been confirmed by
the Minister. Number 14 Mortlock Gardens would thus, the squat-

ters claimed, have a life of over a year, making it usable by squatters.

The council's confidential reply to 'Conspiracy to Deceive' (Members Information Paper no. 13) did not dispute any of the squatters' facts. Indeed, at the council meeting on 17 March, in reply to a further question on the subject from Councillor Percival, Councillor Sawyer admitted that 'the date for the commencement of the demolition of Mortlock Gardens is subject to the confirmation of the Compulsory Purchase Order . . .' (Minutes of Proceedings, page 405).

The council's defence in Members Information Paper no. 13 was simply that Councillor Sawyer did not say 'that 14 Mortlock Gardens is to be demolished in April 1971' as the squatters alleged. Strictly speaking that is correct: it just has to be realized that when Councillor Sawyer says that 'the Council's contractor has stripped out the interior of 14 Mortlock Gardens to prevent its occupation by unauthorized persons' and then continues 'as a demolition contract on the Cossall Street area is due to commence in April or May of this year' he is not referring to the demolition of the Mortlock Gardens part of the site, but to some other part!

Councillor O'Grady's letter

I have referred already to Councillor O'Grady's letter to *The Times* of 18 January, circulated to his staff as Members Information Paper no. 10. In this he divides the empty properties into various categories, one of which shows that 'only 34 properties have been found to be uneconomic to patch repair'. That this statement is quite untrue is, by now, I hope, manifestly obvious. Apart from the Housing and Highways and Works Joint Sub-Committee report of 11 November, which said there were ninety-seven, and the chief executive's report of 30 November which said 'more than 100' and 'estimated' about 130, the Housing (Management) Sub-Committee agenda of 7 January contains a report of the property surveyor listing the addresses of 112 'uneconomic to patch repair' properties.

In 'Conspiracy to Deceive' the squatters accused Councillor O'Grady of lying in his letter to *The Times*. In the council's reply, Information Paper no. 13, dated 16 February 1971, it is 'explained' that this drop from 'more than 100' (Chief Executive's Report 30 November 1970) to thirty-four in Councillor O'Grady's letter to *The Times* also arose from the earmarking of these eighty-five properties for early demolition.

Clearly this explains what the council has *decided to do* with eighty-five of its 'uneconomic to patch repair' properties but it hardly alters the fact that when Councillor O'Grady wrote that 'only thirty-four properties have been found to be uneconomic to patch repair' on 18 January, this was in fact not true.

Further Developments

If, by publishing 'Conspiracy to Deceive', the squatters had hoped that in future statements in the council chamber on empty properties by Councillors O'Grady and Sawyer would be more accurate, then they must have been sorely disillusioned by the council meeting on 17 March 1971. Councillor Richard Percival was again the questioner.

He asked Councillor O'Grady 'whether or not it is true that the Council's policy in relation to properties which are uneconomic to patch repair is to include them as soon as possible in demolition contracts' (Minutes of Proceedings, page 403). If one remembers the chief executive's confidential report of 30 November which said that 'these properties are not within the immediate demolition programme but, where it is practicable to do so steps are being taken to demolish them', or Members Information Paper no. 13, dated 16 February 1971 (confidential) which attempts to explain how 'more than 100' such properties fell to thirty-four because of the 'earmarking of these eighty-five properties for early demolition' then Councillor O'Grady's straight 'No' (Minutes of Proceedings, page 403), in reply to Councillor Percival's question, is somewhat puzzling!

Councillor Percival also questioned Councillor Sawyer – as to how many empty properties in the Consort development area 'are uneconomic to patch repair' (ibid. page 404). When Councillor Sawyer replied that 'only one property has proved uneconomic to patch repair' (ibid. page 405), any observer would probably have been impressed at the extent of the council's use of empty property. It would, then, perhaps have come as a surprise to such an observer to read two confidential documents which Councillor Sawyer would have had in his possession. One has already been referred to – the report of the property surveyor dated 30 November 1970, presented to the Housing (Management) Sub-Committee on 7 January (Document HSG/MAN 15. 70–71. This lists 112 houses found to be uneconomic to patch repair. Of these, eighteen are in Blackpool Road, Claude Road, Consort Road, Phillip Road, Pilkington Road and Manaton Road (all SE 15) – all of which are in the Consort development area.

The second document is the report of the property surveyor dated 14 February 1971 to the Housing (Management) Sub-Committee of 4 March (Document HSG/MAN 19. 70–71). This lists another four houses in Claude Road, Copeland Road, Heaton Road and Grimwade Crescent (all SE 15) which have been found to be uneconomic to patch repair and which are all in the Consort development area.

In all, therefore, twenty-two houses in that area have been found to be uneconomic to patch repair, not one as stated publicly by Councillor Sawyer in the council chamber on 17 March.

Conclusions

It is, I maintain, abundantly clear that Councillors O'Grady and Sawyer have presented false information to the public and to the council. They have deliberately tried to minimize the number of properties that are uneconomic to patch repair. The reasons for doing this are blatantly obvious: if there are no (or few) properties with a reasonable length of life available then there is no room for the squatters in the borough, and their 'hard line' is justifiable. In addition, while giving incorrect information about the number of properties, they have embarked on a policy to try and ensure that their figures do, actually, become correct: by the early demolition of 'uneconomic to patch repair' properties. It is significant that both documents that admit this policy are confidential, whilst Councillor O'Grady denied it in the council chamber.

I submit that the evidence outlined in this appendix shows that these two men have publicly lied and misled the public. The issues at stake are therefore far wider than a few squatters in abandoned houses. The whole concept of democracy, of accountability and of elected representatives' duty to tell the truth to the public and to the council itself has been abused and ignored.

Appendix 2
Southwark Family Squatting Association Press Statement

Open letter to all interested parties 29.12.70

We issue this document because following the decision of the Court of Appeal on 16th December many people have shown great interest in our cause, and have urged the Council to heed the remarks of Lord Justice Edmund Davies, who said that he wished Southwark Council and the Squatters could reach a similar agreement to the 'admirable' one existing in Lewisham.

Indeed, even before his remarks many interested people in the Borough had written to the Council condemning their failure to negotiate a settlement with us. The Council has countered with a number of arguments which are either absolutely invalid or thoroughly dishonest. We seek to answer them here. (We apologise for the length of this statement, but we feel that everybody should know the full details of these affairs.)

1. 'The activities of the Squatters Association will almost certainly result in a large number of "outsiders" coming into Southwark.' (Council Press statement 24.9.70)

This is a statement completely without foundation, and on 25.9.70 we wrote to the Council saying 'there is, however, no evidence that this has happened in Lewisham where a similar scheme has been working successfully.' We reiterate this statement and defy anybody to produce one scrap of evidence to support the Council's argument.

2. 'The number of homeless cases which the Welfare Department might have to deal with could well be doubled or even trebled.' (Council Press statement 24.9.70)

This is utter nonsense. In Lewisham the Lewisham Family Squatting Association have rehoused two families with Court orders against them (Warner and Phillipson, now squatting at 32 Adolphus St., S.E.8.) and one who had been burnt out (Akisanya, now squatting at 34 Amersham Vale S.E.14.) These families would certainly have become the responsibility of the Welfare Department had not the L.F.S.A. existed. In addition, the L.F.S.A. has rehoused many families with court hearings pending – most of whom would almost certainly have ended up at the Welfare Department, had not the L.F.S.A. intervened. Further, a group now set up in Tower Hamlets has reached an agreement in principle with that Council to rehouse families that they would otherwise provide Welfare Accommodation for. Also the Tower Hamlets Family Squatting Association has reached an agreement with Newham Welfare Department to provide temporary accommodation for three families that that Council's Welfare Department would otherwise take.

In Southwark too, our proposed scheme could have a similar effect. Indeed, by evicting the families squatting at the moment and providing them with Welfare accommodation (which they don't want) it is the Council that is overloading its already crowded Welfare homes (which they don't, presumably, want to do).

Their policy is insane from all angles.

3. 'Although the Squatters ... would rehouse only families from the waiting list, it is probable that many of the families thus rehoused would come from a long way down the waiting list. The Council, may, therefore find itself in the position of having to rehouse these families in permanent housing ahead of families whose *present* position on the waiting list is higher.' (Council Press statement 24.9.70)

This argument is not only incorrect – it is thoroughly dishonest, for when putting it forward the Council knew that in Lewisham this was – and still is – not the case. When houses there are required by the Council the families squatting are only rehoused by the Council *if they have come up on the housing list in the normal way* whilst squatting. Those that have not come up are either re-squatted or referred to a housing association by the squatters. We have at present agreements with two – Quadrant and Trinity and we are negotiating with others.

Indeed squatting families, if anything, jump *slightly down* the housing list, because if a family comes to the top of the list whilst squatting we see it as quite reasonable that the Council should *defer* their permanent rehousing until the end of the short-life squatting property they are in. This has happened to about a dozen families in Lewisham.

It is also worth mentioning, in addition, that many of our families in fact do *not* come from a long way down the list. We only squat the most desperate families who are therefore high on the list, but will still have to wait some time for permanent accommodation. This is particularly true in Southwark where the large redevelopment programme (which we applaud) means that most of the houses becoming available at present are needed for families *not* on the waiting list, but whom the Council has to rehouse from clearance areas. (See *The Times* 8.9.70). Thus even families near the top of the list will have to wait some time for permanent rehousing.

4. The squatters' proposals 'would delay the Council's very large housing programme ... (which) depends on having cleared sites, at the right time.' (Council Press statement 24.9.70). The Council statement says that although our undertaking to 'vacate properties when they are required ... might be given in good faith' our ability to keep to this is 'an insecure cornerstone on which to base one of the largest housing programmes in the country'.

This argument is at least logical – but we are bound to point out that it is incorrect. Our record in Southwark alone speaks for itself :

a) On 17.10.70 we squatted Mrs Weekes in 52 Stanbury Road, S.E.15. On hearing from neighbours, however, that this house was going to be used for Old Age Pensioners, we vacated it *next day* and on 18.10.70 moved Mrs Weekes into 19 Tappersfield Road S.E.15. We wrote to the Council pointing this out to them on 18.10.70.

b) In November 1970 we squatted the Flowers family in a house in Peckham Hill Street. A few days later we discovered that this was a G.L.C. house, with whom the Lewisham Squatters have an arrangement for the use of short-life houses. Not wishing to jeopardise this, at the request of County Hall, we voluntarily vacated this house 1 week later.

c) In October 1970 we squatted the Simpson family in 163 Consort Road. At the end of November we discovered that this was an empty privately owned house we had taken by mistake. We vacated the house four days later at the request of the owner.

We are bound to point out that these mistakes only occur where the Council does not co-operate and tell us where its empty houses are. They *never* occur in Lewisham. Mistaken or not, however, they are hardly the actions of a group that has any intention of holding up any plan, breaking agreements or acting irresponsibly.

Our record in other Boroughs is equally impressive :

d) In July 1969 we signed an agreement with the Redbridge

Council to vacate certain houses and not to resume squatting. We have honoured that.

e) In January 1970 we vacated on time two houses when required to by the Lewisham Council. In addition, plans for the clearance of the Adolphus St site in Deptford in March 1971 are already well advanced. Families we will have to re-squat have been given new houses *already*.

f) Between September 1970 and the present day we have intervened in the deadlock between the Arbour Square squatters in Stepney (who were nothing to do with us) and the Tower Hamlets Council and secured a settlement with that Council and with Newham and Camden Welfare Departments, who also have families in Arbour Square, for the peaceful clearance of squatters from there, to avoid modernisation plans being held up. Negotiating with three different Councils was not easy but such is our commitment to the ideas of peaceful constructive settlements and that squatters should not hold up Council plans, that we undertook the task. The result is that an agreement in principle has now been reached with Tower Hamlets Council to set up a Tower Hamlets Family Squatting Association.

No! There is not one iota of evidence to support Southwark's contention that our undertakings are an 'insecure cornerstone' on which to base their building programme. Indeed we will go further than this: not only will we give undertakings to vacate properties in time – but all our families will sign *enforceable legal documents* to this effect as an added guarantee.

These were the main initial objections of the Council to our proposals. We hope that we have shown that these objections, although sometimes logical, are invalid. Indeed we do not criticise the Council for raising objections – it is their duty to consider all angles – but we do criticise them for not withdrawing them when we can show that they are wrong.

Since the Council's press statement of 24.9.70 however, various bodies have written to or contacted the Council protesting at its refusal to reach an agreement with us. Numerous arguments have been used by the Council in an attempt to counter their approaches. We list these arguments and our comments on them here:

5. In its initial Press Statement of 24.9.70, in a letter to the U.G.S. settlement, 16.11.70, in a letter to the Cambridge House and Talbot Settlements, 20.11.70, and in a letter to the Shelter-backed Family Squatting Advisory Service, 16.12.70, the Council has emphasised

that its new policy is to spend more money on short life houses and thus use more properties than in the past, for families off the Council's waiting list, for homeless families and for their 'young couples' scheme. No one in their right mind can oppose this new policy – and we certainly do not. On 25.9.70 we wrote to the Council saying that we 'applaud and support this policy'. Our Press Statement of 1.10.70 said that 'we are very pleased to hear of this change of policy' and on 8.10.70 we even wrote to the Council saying that we would *assist* them in their new policy – by placing our resources at the disposal of any 'young couples' who take short-life houses (under the Council's new plan they will be responsible for their own repairs). Indeed when our representatives, Messrs Stone, Bailey, Peters and Lyndsay met the Council (Messrs Evans, O'Grady and Halford) on 20th October 1970 they even offered to arrange to have the 20 worst houses repaired *at our expense* for the Southwark Welfare Dept to use.

Under their new scheme the Council will thus use the best of the empty houses – rightly so. What we have repeatedly said is that we will use some of the rest. Our letter to the Council of 25.9.70. said 'we are interested in those that would still cost you too much to use'. Our Press Statement of 1.10.70. urged the Council to 'tell us which houses they do not intend to use' under the new scheme and said that 'we will make them habitable'. Our letter to the Council of 8.10.70 called for a 'joint effort' to get as much property as possible into use.

The houses we are interested in are, we repeat, those which the Council will not use under its new scheme; houses like 14, Mortlock Gardens S.E.15 which, on 4th November 1970 at 3.00 p.m. Council workmen entered and wrecked the inside of – smashing the sink, the toilet, the window frames, the banisters, ripping out the piping and fireplace. Dozens of other houses in Cliffton Way, Cliffton Crescent, King Alfred's Way, Harders Road etc. have suffered similarly: and all of them have at least a year's life. And we have *photographs* to prove these allegations. O.K., so the damage has now been done ('rat prevention' the Council calls it): the Council does not want to use these houses. We do: we'll repair them at our expense! What possible objections can the Council have to such an offer?

6. The Council is now alleging that we are delaying their plans to bring more houses into use under their new scheme. In their letters already mentioned to the U.G.S. Settlement, 16.11.70, the Cambridge House and Talbot Settlements, 20.11.70, and the Family

Squatting Advisory Service, 16.12.70, they have made the following accusations:

a) that one of the first houses to be 'patch repaired' under the Council's new policy has been occupied by us, thus preventing them from using it, and

b) three of the houses we are occupying are due to be converted into six dwellings, so we are thus delaying the rehousing of six families who have waited patiently for years.

These are cunning arguments but they are *thoroughly dishonest to the core*, and show that the Council has no genuine logical arguments on which to base its anti-squatter policy, but is merely seeking to prevent support for the squatters growing by means of *dishonest* tactics. Let us examine these allegations that the Council have made.

It is possible that the two accusations are, speaking strictly, true (although this will not be known for certain until the Council publishes a list of all empty properties it has considered under its new scheme listing those they intend to use and those that they have rejected) and that we *are* in fact occupying one of their 'patch repaired' houses and three houses that they intend to convert into six dwellings. It is possible, we admit that: but if it is true then we categorically state that it is *not our fault but the Council's.*

We will explain why.

We have repeatedly stated that if we have occupied any house that the Council intends to use, then all they have to do is to tell us which ones, and we will move out (quite voluntarily: no Court Orders needed) and into houses that they do not intend to use. Our letter to the Council of 25.9.72. stated quite explicity: 'Let us say here and now that you do not need Court Orders or proceedings to get us out. All you need is to demonstrate that you will use the houses – by sending your workmen to repair them rather than destroy them ... simply show us that you will ... install families in the houses that we occupy, and let us know which houses that you will not use so that we can move to them, and we will, as always, vacate the houses when you require them.'

We said that *over three months ago* on 25th September and we say it again now. For three months the Council have ignored it.

Again on 30th September we wrote to the Council that 'if you require any of the nine houses that squatters now occupy we will move to a house that you do not require.' This was again ignored. Our Press Statement of 1st October was equally clear: 'We would like to say as we have said all along that the Council do not need

Court Orders to make our families leave. All we ask is that the Council let us rehouse those and other families in houses that they never intend to use.'

When the Blackfriars Settlement approached the Council they made the same offer; on 2nd December when the U.G.S. Settlement wrote to the Council they also pointed out that this was a strict policy of ours.

If then we are inadvertently occupying one house that the Council has 'patch repaired' and three others that they intend to convert into six units, then it is *simply and solely* because the Council has consistently ignored all our offers to voluntarily vacate houses if they will only tell us which ones they require. We can only come to the conclusion that the Council actually wants us to remain in houses that they require for a while, so that they can claim, absolutely dishonestly, that we are preventing them from using houses. It is therefore the *fault of the Council* if we are in any way delaying the rehousing of families by them.

But our offer still stands: we will vacate houses that they need and move to ones that they do not intend to use. And our actions already mentioned at Stanbury Road, Peckham Hill Street and Consort Road show that we are both sincere in making this offer and able to carry it out.

7. In the letter to the Family Squatting Advisory Service of 16.12.70 the Council claimed that we have squatted families not on the Council's housing waiting list, 'which contrasts sharply with the Southwark Squatters' Association's proposals'. In reply we would mention the following points:

a) If we have squatted families not on the housing list, all of them were certainly the *welfare responsibility* of the Council as they were homeless in the Borough. We did not bring them to Southwark.

b) How, anyway, do the Council expect us to be able to check up who is on their housing list when they do not co-operate with us. In Lewisham, where the Council does co-operate, the squatters can and do check with the Housing Dept. so the problem does not arise. If Southwark would also co-operate we too would only rehouse families in consultation with the Housing Dept.

c) We have stated that if the Council would come to an agreement with us we would only rehouse families from the housing list after consultation with the Housing Department. As the Council have *not* come to an agreement we are under no such obligation, although even now we have voluntarily limited ourselves to families that are either the housing or the welfare responsibility of this Borough.

We repeat: we want to come to a similar arrangement with the Southwark Council to the ones we have reached with Lewisham, Tower Hamlets, Greenwich and the G.L.C. and which many other Councils are now showing an interest in (e.g. Redbridge, Hackney, Brent, Waltham Forest etc.).

We do not particularly want a victory in Southwark: we want a constructive settlement to get houses into use. In order to achieve this we are prepared to make compromises: we appeal to the Council to do the same.

Can we suggest negotiations along these lines, perhaps conducted through an impartial third party (or parties). Surely this is preferable to evictions, empty houses, house wrecking and a continued waste of effort in conflict?

Penguinews *and* Penguins in Print

Every month we issue an illustrated magazine, *Penguinews*. It's a lively guide to all the latest Penguins, Pelicans and Puffins, and always contains an article on a major Penguin author, plus other features of contemporary interest.

Penguinews is supplemented by *Penguins in Print*, a complete list of all the available Penguin titles – there are now over four thousand!

The cost is no more than the postage; so why not write for a free copy of this month's *Penguinews*? And if you'd like both publications sent for a year, just send us a cheque or a postal order for 30p (if you live in the United Kingdom) or 60p (if you live elsewhere), and we'll put you on our mailing list.

Dept EP, Penguin Books Ltd,
Harmondsworth, Middlesex

Note: *Penguinews* and *Penguins in Print* are not available in the U.S.A. or Canada

Another Penguin Special

The Penguin Guide to Supplementary Benefits

Tony Lynes

Supplementary benefits (once called National Assistance) and the newer and more clear-cut family income supplements exist as a safety-net for those who fall between the various benefits of national insurance or below a certain minimum level of income. They are paid at the discretion of the Supplementary Benefits Commission . . . but how that discretion will be exercised (through local offices) is very hard to say.

This is a simple, comprehensive and up-to-date guide to the grounds on which claims can be based, to the likely response of local officials and to the machinery for appealing against first decisions. By explaining the guide-lines put down by the Commission and examining the awards granted in certain cases, Tony Lynes helps to clarify the official attitude to rents, clothing, heating and other necessities and to such 'extras' as hire-purchase, holidays and even telephones.

There is little that is cut and dried either in the entitlement to or the award of supplementary benefits. This handbook does much to simplify the picture, both for claimants and for those who act professionally or voluntarily for them.